GW00725874

JOHN HENRY NEWMAN:
UNIVERSAL REVELATION

JOHN HENRY NEWMAN:
UNIVERSAL REVELATION

FRANCIS McGRATH, F.M.S.

With a Foreword by
GERARD TRACEY

BURNS & OATES

JOHN GARRATT PUBLISHING

First published in Great Britain in 1997 by
BURNS & OATES,
Wellwood, North Farm Road,
Tunbridge Wells, Kent TN2 3DR

Published in Australia in 1997 by
John Garratt Publishing
32 Glenvale Crescent,
Mulgrave, Victoria, 3170

ISBN (UK) 0 86012 273 5
ISBN (Australia) 1 875938 30 3

The National Library of Australia Cataloguing-in-Publication data:

McGrath, Francis J., 1935-.
  John Henry Newman: Universal Revelation.

  Bibliography.
  Includes index.
  ISBN 1 875938 30 3

  1. Newman, John Henry. 1801-1890. 2. Catholic Church -
Clergy - Biography. 3. Cardinals - England - Biography. 4.
Church and state - Great Britain - History. I. Title.

282.092

Typeset by Search Press Limited
Printed in Great Britain by Biddles Ltd,
Guildford and King's Lynn

Contents

Abbreviations

Abbreviations used for works by Newman are those listed in Joseph Rickaby, S.J., *Index to the Works of John Henry Cardinal Newman* (London, 1914), with some additions. Unless otherwise stated, references to works included by Newman in the uniform edition are always to that edition, which began in 1868 with *Parochial and Plain Sermons* and which concluded in 1881 with *Select Treatises of St Athanasius*.

Apo.	*Apologia pro Vita Sua*
Ari.	*The Arians of the Fourth Century*
Ath., I, II	*Selected Treatises of St Athanasius*, 2 volumes
A.W.	*John Henry Newman: Autobiographical Writings*
Call.	*Callista: a Tale of the Third Century*
D.A.	*Discussions and Arguments on Various Subjects*
Dev.	*An Essay on the Development of Christian Doctrine*
Diff., I, II	*Certain Difficulties felt by Anglicans in Catholic Teaching*, 2 volumes
Ess., I, II	*Essays Critical and Historical*, 2 volumes
G.A.	*An Essay in Aid of a Grammar of Assent*
H.S., I, II	*Historical Sketches*, 3 volumes
Idea	*The Idea of a University defined and illustrated*
Jfc.	*Lectures on the Doctrine of Justification*
K.C.	*Correspondence of John Henry Newman with John Keble and Others, 1839-1845*
L.G.	*Loss and Gain: the Story of a Convert*
M.D.	*Meditations and Devotions of the late Cardinal Newman*
Mir.	*Two Essays on Biblical and on Ecclesiastical Miracles*
Mix.	*Discourses addressed to Mixed Congregations*
Moz., I, II	*Letters and Correspondence of John Henry Newman*, 2 volumes
O.S.	*Sermons preached on Various Occasions*

P.S., I-VIII	*Parochial and Plain Sermons*
Prepos.	*Present Position of Catholics*
S.D.	*Sermons bearing on Subjects of the Day*
S.E.	*Stray Essays on Controversial Points*
S.N.	*Sermons Notes of John Henry Cardinal Newman, 1849-1878*
T.T.	*Tracts Theological and Ecclesiastical*
U.S.	*Fifteen Sermons preached before the University of Oxford*
V.M.	*The Via Media*, 2 volumes
V.V.	*Verses on Various Occasions*

* * *

A.S., I, II	*Anglican Sermons*, 2 volumes
L.D., I-XXXI	*The Letters and Diaries of John Henry Newman*
T.P., I, II	*The Theological Papers of John Henry Newman*, 2 volumes
P.N., I, II	*John H. Newman, The Philosophical Notebook*, 2 volumes

* * *

ANCL	*Ante-Nicene Christian Library*
BOA	Birmingham Oratory Archives

At the beginning of time, as God's Spirit moved over the waters, God began to communicate something of God's goodness and beauty to all creation. When God then created man and woman, God gave them the good things of the earth for their use and benefit; and God put into their hearts abilities and powers, which were God's gifts. And to all human beings throughout the ages God has given a desire for the Godhead, *a desire which different cultures have tried to express in their own ways. . . .**

But for thousands of years you have lived in this land and fashioned a culture that endures to this day. And during all this time, the Spirit of God has been with you. Your "Dreaming," which influences your lives so strongly that, no matter what happens, you remain forever people of your culture, is *your own way of touching the mystery of God's Spirit** in you and in creation. You must keep your striving for God and hold on to it in your lives. . . .

Some of the stories from your Dreamtime legends speak powerfully of the great mysteries of human life, its frailty, its need for help, its closeness to spiritual powers, and the value of the human person. They are not unlike some of the great inspired lessons from the people among whom Jesus himself was born. It is wonderful to see how people, as they accept the gospel of Jesus, find *points of agreement between their own traditions and those of Jesus and his people.**

(From John Paul II's address to Australian Aborigines and Torres Strait Islanders at Blatherskite Park, Alice Springs, Northern Territory, Australia, 29 November 1986. *Pope's emphasis)

*To my parents
Eileen Margaret and William Robert
with love and gratitude*

Foreword

It is a great pleasure to have been asked to write a foreword to Dr McGrath's new work, which takes up the challenging observation of the late Father Stephen Dessain concerning the lack of any study of Newman's understanding of revelation and its existence outside Christianity.

John Henry Newman: the starting point for any study of the life and thought of this great man of God has to be the first conversion he underwent at the age of fifteen. That momentous experience, which he considered to have been a turning-round of his whole life by God, left him under the influence of a definite creed, containing the essential truths of the Christian faith. The influence of Thomas Scott ensured that the doctrine of the Holy Spirit was embraced in all its fullness, along with the other "great and burning" truths that were to remain impressed upon Newman's heart for the rest of his life. Ordination was to lead him to adjust his view of the practical and pastoral application of the saving truths he had learnt in his youth. Others were to help him to balance his perception of the relationship between scripture and tradition. The office of the Church in the Christian religion was to become clearer over the years.

Christianity, then, was for Newman a revealed religion carrying at its heart certain definite truths concerning a loving creator God. But all men are created. What of those men who have no access to the doctrines that tell something of God's personality, will, and plan for us? While the young and zealous Evangelical Newman may have made some allowance for those born under the incomplete dispensation of Judaism, the heathen world was one of darkness, devoid of any revelation whatsoever. Within barely five years, however, Newman was to declare: "I believe in an *universal* revelation—the doctrines of which are preserved by tradition in the world at large."

Dr McGrath's penetrating study examines this momentous development and goes on to suggest answers to many related questions. The Newman of the first conversion is considered with care, together with the evangelical teaching he absorbed. Newman remarked in the *Apologia* that during his mid-twenties he was "drifting in the direction of the liberalism of the day." Rather than just repeating Newman's own description, Dr McGrath examines the details of this hiatus in Newman's recovery of the full circle of Christian doctrine. Newman's three different forays into patristic studies between 1828 and 1835 were to yield varying amounts of fruit. It was his study of the Alexandrian Fathers that was to be of crucial significance, and Dr McGrath provides a concise and helpful explanation of their theology, giving a fresh perspective on the little recognized influence of Justin Martyr and his concept of a "*Logos spermatikos.*"

Newman never wrote without a call. With the exception of the *Grammar of Assent*, all his writings were occasional. Dr McGrath's study reveals how the challenge of liberalism goaded Newman into refining his theology of revelation, and how it was the liberal Anglican H. H. Milman's *History of Christianity* that led Newman to declare that "from the beginning the Moral Governor of the World has scattered the seeds of truth far and wide overs its extent," and to elaborate upon the implications of this statement.

The development of doctrine and the inspiration of scripture are subjects of central concern to the Christian theologian. Newman's *Essay of Development* is well known, but he also had much to say on biblical theology that, while often only inchoate, is insightful and germane. Dr McGrath brings these disparate sources to light. He also addresses Newman's analysis of the relationship between the manifest and the mysterious components of revelation, without balking at the difficult definition of what constitutes "a mystery" in theology. Later theologians have addressed this whole area with more system and method than Newman, and the conclusion to Dr McGrath's study examines the extent to which Newman's theology of revelation can be said to be in harmony with the more significant figures in twentieth-century theology, both Catholic and Protestant.

Dr McGrath is to be congratulated warmly. In this seminal work he has utilized all sources—primary and secondary, printed and manuscript—with thoroughness and a keenly perceptive eye. While Dr McGrath's commentary is shrewd and his exposition clear, Newman's own words are allowed to breathe by means of ample quotation. There is much of interest and profit here for Newman scholars and a wider readership alike.

Gerard Tracy
The Oratory, Birmingham, August 1997

Preface

Tracing the development of Newman's understanding of revelation involved utilizing the full range of primary sources housed in the Birmingham Oratory Archives. This meant working through the uniform edition of Newman's works, first editions, posthumous editions, critical editions, plus the *Letters and Diaries*. Just as importantly, it also meant chronologically reading his unpublished Anglicans sermons, his unpublished theological papers, letters, diaries, and memoranda. Secondary sources included those individuals who influenced his early views on revelation in the wake of his Evangelical conversion, including Thomas Scott and Daniel Wilson, and those who influenced his later views, including Justin Martyr, Clement of Alexandria, and Bishop Joseph Butler. Then, there were the writings of prominent liberal Anglicans who were to have a catalytic effect on his polemical style and his thinking on revelation, including Renn Dickson Hampden, Baden Powell, Richard Whately, Joseph Blanco White, and Henry Hart Milman, in addition to an American Congregationalist minister by the name of Jacob Abbott and two Scottish churchmen—Thomas Chalmers of Glasgow and Thomas Erskine of Linlathen.

The research and writing of this book has taken many years and, along the way, a lot of people have contributed to the project by way of material and moral support, when the going got tough, particularly when the going got tough!

First of all, I am deeply grateful for the ongoing support and interest of my sisters, Clare and Aileen, and for the support of my brothers, Michael, William, and John throughout the whole project.

To fellows members of the Sydney province of Marist Brothers in Australia, I am also grateful. First of all, my thanks to a former provincial, Alman Dwyer FMS, and to the present incumbent, Michael Hill FMS. I would then like to thank my present community at Marist College Ashgrove, Brisbane, who left me alone to get on with the job. In particular, I thank Flavian Field FMS, Cyrus Callaghan FMS, Robert McArthur FMS, Patrick Butler FMS, and Dignam Vianney FMS. I would also like to acknowledge the support and encouragement of the late Wayne Duncan FMS.

I also thank the Brisbane Education Centre for its support and encouragement. First of all, special thanks to my partner on the *Foundations* programme, John Coles; and thanks then to Pam Betts, Madonna Botting, Dianne Goosem, Tim Keating, Ron McKeirnan, Margaret O'Reilly, Vince O'Rourke, Leo Power, Nick Ryan, and Pauline Smoothy RSM. Also, my thanks to Mary McNeill, Diane Stark and the secretarial team; and last, but by no means least, my thanks to Gai Mason and her ever courteous printery staff.

I am also grateful to Edmund Campion, Chair of the Literature Fund of the Australia Council, for his useful comments and encouragement.

No preface can be complete without mentioning the enormous support I received from the Great Britain province of Marist Brothers, particularly the community at Old Fallings Lane, Wolverhampton, who warmly welcomed a stranger from Down Under into their midst. My thanks especially go to Dominic Dickins FMS, John Patrick FMS, Patrick Shiels FMS, Henry Jackson FMS, the late Godric John Smith FMS, and the late Anastasius Patrick Bradley FMS. I also thank their lifelong friend and affiliated member, Phyllis Williams, together with the Business Education Centre at Our Lady and St Chad Comprehensive School, Wolverhampton.

My thanks also go to the Master and Fellows of Campion Hall, Oxford, particularly to my hall supervisor, the late James O'Higgins S.J., and to Anthony Meredith S.J. I am further indebted to Geoffrey Rowell, formerly of Keble College, to John Macquarrie, Emeritus Lady Margaret Professor of Divinity, and to Maurice Wiles, Regius Professor of Divinity, Christ Church.

To the Fathers of the Birmingham Oratory, to their present superior, the Very Reverend Paul Chavasse, and to his predecessor, Gregory Winterton, I express my appreciation for their hospitality over many years, for giving me access to the Newman Archives and Library, and for permission to reproduce the material in the book. I also thank Jean Pearson and Fred Fitzpatrick for their invaluable assistance as the project neared completion.

Finally, my deepest thanks must go to the current librarian and archivist at the Birmingham Oratory, Gerard Tracey, who is also the current editor of the *Letters and Diaries of John Henry Newman*. I shall always be grateful for his unstinting support, encouragement and constructive comments and criticisms which, as usual, have been "spot on." Most of all, I am indebted to him for sharing his unique and encyclopaedic knowledge of Newman and of the amazing age he lived in.

F.McG. 11 August 1997.

Introduction

The eminent Newman scholar Charles Stephen Dessain once remarked that there exists no full study of Newman's understanding of revelation and its existence outside Christianity. In the hope of making up for such an omission, this book attempts to trace the development of Newman's thought on the subject from his early Evangelical years, through those of the Tractarian movement, and the second half of his life, when he was a Roman Catholic. It further examines four related themes: external and internal evidences for revelation; revelation and development; revelation and mystery; revelation and inspiration. Newman always thought of himself as "a controversialist, not a theologian."[1] He was never called upon to draw up a systematic study of revelation. What he said (and that was a good deal, and much of great value) is dispersed throughout his works—sermons, essays and letters. It is not only possible to recover his understanding of the universal aspect of revelation, but also possible to hint, in broad outline, at the story of his theological development over a sixty-year period. It should be stated from the outset that, for reason of length if no other, this study is expository rather than analytical.

As a result of his Evangelical conversion, he "fell under the influences of a definite Creed" and received into his "intellect impressions of dogma" that were to last the rest of his life.[2] Soon after ordination, he was drawn into a lengthy argument about revelation with his brother Charles, who had announced his abandonment of Christianity. For Charles, revelation was full of lies and Christians a pack of fools for believing them. Following this debate by letter, Newman announced a series of sermons on revelation and these constitute his first exploration of the area. Not that it was a particularly fruitful exercise, because he was theologically unprepared, and relied too heavily on other authors, particularly Daniel Wilson and Thomas Erskine. Not surprisingly, the centre of attention is the atonement—the cornerstone of the revealed system according to Evangelicals. Judaism and Christianity are presented as the only two "dispensations" with a legitimate claim to a divine revelation. All others in the world were simply examples of permanent alienation from a just and loving God.

Even before relinquishing his curacy at St Clement's and accepting a tutorship at Oriel College, Newman began to drift away from Evangelicalism and toward an anti-dogmatic liberalism whose "characteristic aspect" was a "cold Arminian doctrine," typical of the "Oriel divines."[3] Several sermons of this period, particularly those on the Trinity and the mediatorship of Christ, were suggestively liberal or, as he retrospectively labelled them, "Whatelyan." He was "rudely" woken from this flirtation by "two great blows—illness and bereavement."[4] Both factors, in conjunction with his reading of the early Church Fathers and Bishop Butler, steered him into the mainstream of orthodoxy and enabled him to "complete his recovery of the full Christian revelation."[5] Although he makes no mention in the *Apologia*, it is almost certain that Justin Martyr's idea of the "*Logos spermatikos*" introduced him to the idea of a universal revelation. In reading Butler's *Sermons*, Newman quickly made the connection between revelation and personal conscience. Personal conscience was, he discovered, one of the principal channels through which God had disclosed himself to every person, in every culture and every age, from time immemorial, independently of Judaism and Christianity. Clement of Alexandria's influence came a little later, while he was preparing to write *Arians of the Fourth Century*.

The Oxford Movement began as a protest against government interference in Church affairs. As Whig political power declined, attention was turned to current liberal Anglicans who were whittling away revealed doctrinal truths without challenge. Most of them maintained religion to contain comparatively little positive truth; that, indeed, one creed may be as good as another; that doctrines should be conformable to strict rules of reasoning; that no external authority has the right to interfere with private judgment; that particular articles of the creed, such as the Trinity, are, at root, human speculations, carrying no guarantee of authenticity. At heart lay the fact, nature and extent of revelation. Hence, much of what Newman had to say on the subject was framed as a response to liberals such as Hampden, Whately, and Blanco White, and to ultra-Protestants such as Erskine.

In 1834 Hampden published a pamphlet urging the admission of dissenters into Oxford. For him, dissent did not involve essential doctrines of Anglicanism, but questions of interpretation. Most people were in basic agreement on the fundamental teachings of Christianity. He could see little reason for people not to worship together. He sent a copy to Newman, who later described it as "the beginning of hostilities in the University."[6] Almost certainly with Hampden in mind, Newman composed five sermons, which, collectively, represent one of his earliest sustained defences of the dogmatic principle and, indeed, are the only five sermons he wrote specifically for publication rather than for the pulpit.

He had already warned about Whately's *Omission of Creeds* in 1832, and Hampden's nomination to the Regius Professorship of Divinity in 1836 made Newman more visible and vocal in opposing Anglican liberalism. Blanco White's recent rejection of Christianity would have hardened his resolve. During the next six or seven years his thinking on revelation matured, his theological horizons broadened, his language grew sharper, his tone more authoritative, his insights more incisive.[7]

Initially, he was content to explain the notion of a universal revelation without having to defend it. With liberal Anglicans questioning the position of sacraments and various doctrines in relation to any certain revealed system, particularly if their origins could be traced back to non-Christian sources, Newman's response was to argue that these were some of the reasons why they are part of the revealed word of God. Indeed, such was the amazing assimilative power of Christianity.

In the Catholic years, Newman continued to talk of the universal aspects of revelation on many occasions. God was the source of everything and everywhere that was good, true and beautiful. Nature and grace work hand in hand. Virgil possessed prophetic gifts and Xenophon was one of the most religious of writers. While the Church is the ordinary channel of revelation, art, music, literature, philosophy, and the Koran are also channels. Of all subjects, this one especially fascinated him.

Like many others of his day, the young Newman accepted Paley's classic argument from design as a sufficient proof for the existence of God. But he came to perceive its inherent weakness and preferred to focus on personal, internal evidence (proof) for belief. The source of one's faith will always remain beyond reason but can never be against it. Natural religion supplies each and every one of us with certain information about God and our responsibilities toward him. Such information concerning God generally comes in one of three ways: through the collective voice of humanity, through the history of the world, or through the mind of the individual. Of these channels, the most authoritative is the individual mind, which supplies the criteria by which we test, interpret, and correct the testimony of the human race and the history of the world. The most reliable internal mentor is personal conscience, which not only teaches that God exists, but impresses upon our imagination the image of a supreme judge who is holy, just and powerful, and is the creative principle of religion. Of all dispensations, Christianity possesses unique credentials. Rather than supersede natural religion, it builds on it.

As an Anglican Evangelical, Newman had a confident belief in a dogmatic form of Christianity. Later, he became equally confident that a visible Church equipped with sacraments and rites, was an essential feature of "Apostolical Christianity." This was a view rejected by many Protestants, but, he also thought, one corrupted by Roman Catholics. Anglicanism had successfully steered a middle course. But he came to see how impossible it was to steer such a course without some reference to the distinctive principles of Roman Catholicism, especially the sacraments. On this issue, Newman's brother Francis took issue with him, suggesting that there was no more authority for his "Apostolical Christianity" than for contemporary Roman Catholicism. Prompted by this allegation, Newman began, for the first time, to tease out a theory of doctrinal development to show that the doctrines of the Church were authentic developments, rather than corruptions, of Christ's original teaching. While he harboured reservations about the Church of Rome, he now came to have clear reservations about the Church of England, albeit different ones. By the time he wrote *Essay on the Development of Christian Doctrine* in 1845, his reservations about Rome had almost vanished, but not to the extent that he did not need to test his theory of development to see if it could, indeed, account for the doctrines and practices found in the whole history of the Church from Christ's time to the present.

The person of Jesus Christ is a revelation so rich, so complex and so powerful that all subsequent religious doctrines are the Church's ongoing attempt to express particular aspects of that one revelation in human language. It was given once and for all in Jesus and subsequent doctrines are elaborations of the one revelation.

The Evangelical Newman saw revelation as a "manifestation" of divine truths—that is, a clear-cut corpus of intelligible truths. He paid scant attention to the idea of religious mystery but, under the influence of the early Church Fathers, he began to appreciate more and more that "manifestation" and "mystery" are integral components of the same revealed truth; that revelation is "religious doctrine viewed on its illuminated side," and mystery is the "selfsame doctrine viewed on the side unilluminated."[8] One of the tasks of a theologian is to establish, as clearly as possible, what in fact does, and what does not, constitute religious mystery. Since Christianity contains much that is "above," though not "against," reason, it follows that there are many issues that are, humanly speaking, "insoluble."[9]

Some educated Christians of the period began to experience a crisis of faith as the new sciences cast doubt on the plenary inspiration of scripture. The crisis was not so acute for Roman Catholics, who had an external, infallible guide, but it was critical for many Protestants, who had principally only themselves and the Bible to fall back on. In the early 1860s

Newman began work on a detailed examination of biblical inspiration (with a view to a book, which was never to eventuate). As with religious mysteries, he wanted to make clear what the early Fathers and the Church had said on the matter and also what Catholics were bound to believe. He found both sources upheld his own view - namely, that the Bible is inspired as a channel of divine revelation in matters concerning faith and morals, and does not have to be held accountable for inaccuracies in ancillary historical matters. His last publication was also on inspiration and his aim was to keep the issue open as far as possible. By then he was eighty-four years old and a cardinal, and he wished to use his unexpected position to show Catholics that scripture and biblical scholarship did not have to be irreconcilable.

Like most of his contemporaries, Newman's thoughts on revelation were scattered and unsystematic. Under the initiative of Protestant writers such as Karl Barth, twentieth-century theologians have addressed themselves in much more detail to the fact, nature, and extent of revelation. Despite differences of terminology, Newman's thoughts on a universal component of revelation run almost parallel to those of Hans Urs von Balthasar, Karl Rahner and H. Richard Niebuhr. Furthermore, on this issue, as on many others, the Second Vatican Council seems to have taken on the heart and the mind of Newman.

Notes

1. *L.D.* XXII, 157; letter to W. G. Ward (18 Feb. 1866). "I fancy I write better," Newman told Lord Edward Howard in 1864, "when I am led to write by what comes my way" (*L.D.* XXI, 178).
2. *Apo.*, p. 4.
3. *Ibid.*, p. 14; *A.W.*, p. 83.
4. *Ibid.*
5. C. S. Dessain, *John Henry Newman*, p. 11.
6. *L.D.* IV, 371.
7. *Apo.*, p. 93.
8. *Ess.* I, 41.
9. *P.N.* II, 101; 103.

PART I

A DEVELOPING
UNDERSTANDING OF
DIVINE REVELATION

CHAPTER 1

An Anglican Evangelical

Prior to his "Evangelical" conversion of 1816 Newman had "no formed religious convictions."[1] He grew up in an Anglican household where the religion practised was a "bible religion," which consisted of reading scripture either in church, with the family, or privately, and involved no "rites or creeds."[2] He always cherished memories of the Fulham home of his grandmother and Aunt Elizabeth, with whom he frequently stayed as a child. Such was the impact of those visits that he could say forty years later that whatever good was in him he owed to those visits. Nor did he forget his grandmother's illustrated Bible. "I am what I am, and I have grown into what I am from that time at Fulham."[3] As a child, he boasted of a "perfect knowledge" of the catechism, although he had little understanding of its meaning.[4]

By the age of fourteen, he was reading Voltaire, Hume's essays, and Paine's objections to divine revelation. He later remembered copying out "some French verses, perhaps Voltaire's, in denial of the immortality of the soul," and being fascinated by their plausibility.[5] By that stage, he was growing into a highly intelligent, imaginative, but by no means overly religious adolescent.

The conversion, when it did come, was to a moderate form of Calvinistic Evangelicalism and was, for him, the most significant religious event of his life. He became aware of a special bond between himself and God. Such as it was available to him, he "fell under the influences of a definite Creed" and discovered the idea of a dogmatic principle.[6] At the time he was seriously ill and was haunted by "experiences before and after, awful, and known only to God."[7] By his side throughout the crisis was Walter Mayers, his Evangelical classics master, whom he later described as the "human means of this beginning of divine faith" in him. He was even more impressed by the books Mayers gave him to read, mostly from the "school of Calvin," including Thomas Scott, whose writings made a "deeper impression" than anything else and to whom, "humanly speaking," he owed his soul.[8] He was also fascinated by the figures of Augustine and Ambrose in Milner's *History of the Church of Christ*. This was an Evangelical interpre-

tation of the history of "REAL Christians," irrespective of "what EX-
TERNAL Church" they belonged to.[9] Thus it was as a committed Anglican Evangelical that Newman went up to Oxford in June 1817.

Anglicanism was able to assimilate Evangelicalism into the mainstream
of British society in the early part of the nineteenth century. Almost as a
matter of course, people started to refer to Anglican "Evangelicals" as if
they were the main type. They were not numerically strong, but what they
lacked in numbers they more than compensated for in holiness, integrity,
superior organizing skills, and money. As a result, they developed into the
"most dynamic and ambitious element in the Established Church."[10] They
undertook extensive philanthropic work among the poor, trained missionaries and went into publishing. Their infectious enthusiasm was a refresh-
ing contrast to the often lethargic religion of the establishment. Instead of
an impersonal, remote, unattractive God, they preached about a personal,
directly knowable Saviour who was "busy in and among His creation,"
providentially intervening, answering prayers, and performing miracles.[11]
Holiness was their goal and they put it within reach of ordinary Christians.
They preached a "clear-cut" creed about the Fall, the atonement, redemption, and regeneration.[12]

Generally speaking, Anglican Evangelicals were loyal church-goers.
The Thirty-nine Articles were "an almost perfect summary of faith."[13] Of
particular importance was the "great invisible Church of Christ" to which
God's privileged elect belonged by the grace of conversion and the power
of the Holy Spirit.[14] They were "real" Christians of the invisible Church as
compared to "nominal" Christians who, through baptism, belonged to the
visible Church, which had no "inherent power to regenerate or sanctify."
It merely provided a suitable environment where people met for mutual
support and instruction.[15] God's ways of leading people into the "paths of
righteousness" were not normally via sacraments, nor accomplished by
faithful obedience to church authority any more than by regular church
attendance.[16] But justification, conversion, and holiness were the means
and they were "affairs of the Holy Spirit and the individual soul." If there
is a "mediator in the process," it is scripture, which is the "visible expression of God's will." On its own, the visible Church is of "little importance." It is a "pale, earthly shadow" of the invisible Church to which only
God's privileged elect belonged.[17]

Foremost among Newman's Evangelical influences was Thomas Scott,
who suggested dogma as the basis for religion, who insisted on the need for
holiness, and who inculcated a "zealous faith" in the Trinity.[18] Christ is the
"centre of revelation" in whom "all the lines meet from every part of its

ample circumference" and whose atonement, resurrection, and ascension represent the "central" doctrines of revelation.[19] Since scripture is "unanswerably" the revealed word of God, Christians must "reason from it, as from self-evident principles."[20] No one is a true believer "who only holds those doctrines which he regards as the dictates of reason as well as of revelation" and who "rejects the testimony of God, whenever he *deems it unreasonable*." It is dangerously "subversive of revelation" to belittle doctrinal truth. If we really believe that the scriptures are divinely inspired, then "it is the height of arrogance to speak of any doctrine contained in them as false or doubtful, because it does not coincide with our reasonings or conceptions."[21] The appropriate behaviour for a true believer must be full "submission to the will and authority of God" in fear and love.[22] Revealed truth is the "seed" in the soul from which "real holiness" springs.[23]

William Romaine and Bishop Beveridge taught Newman about predestination and human corruption. Although he was to reject predestination within five years, the impression of human corruption lasted longer. One of his earliest sermons was on that subject and he re-preached it seven times over the next seventeen years, each time going out of his way to quote Beveridge on the sinfulness of practically everything we said, did, or thought.[24] Not only did William Law teach him about the "warfare between the city of God and the powers of darkness," but he seems to have played a part in Newman's decision to lead a celibate life, because it was a safer and a speedier road to holiness.[25] William Wilberforce's *Practical Christianity* for "real" Christians, reconfirmed his Evangelicalism.[26] When tackling sermon writing for the first time he turned to Charles Simeon's *Helps to Composition*. His earliest treatment of conscience belongs in a sermon preached on 19 June 1825. In it, he incorporated part of Simeon's skeleton sermon on "A Good and Evil Conscience."[27]

A view of Newman's Evangelicalism can be gained from early sermons and previous private theological papers drawn up between 1821 and 1823.[28] For him the "keystone" of revealed truth is the "infinite enormity of sin, the corruption of the human heart, and the weakness of man's reason." If these are removed, then the whole edifice will collapse. Remove the Ninth Article and the first part of the Tenth, and the Thirty-nine Articles collapse.[29] Human nature, which is "filthy" and "desperately wicked," is utterly incapable of obeying God's unalterable law. Then, when everything looks utterly hopeless, God suddenly unveils a "stupendous scheme" of salvation to this outlawed, disinherited race, some of whom are predestined for paradise while the rest are earmarked for "righteous punishment and merited condemnation."[30]

To save the elect, God is revealed as "a covenanted God" who is much more "inviting" and "endearing" than the stern, forbidding God of the Old Testament. By entering into a personal relationship with some of us, the God of the New Testament reveals the Trinity, in which each person carries out specific tasks to smooth the way for reconciliation with the Father. That is why Christ established his "mediatorial" Kingdom, sacrificed himself for us, died the ignominious death of a sinner, and reconciled a "rebellious and ungodly race" to the Father.[31] Our "only hope of safety and ground of confidence" is to "submit ourselves" as subjects of that Kingdom, which is for saints, not sinners. We can "approach God" only through Jesus Christ. As we do, we do not plead "*our* merits but *His*." Nor do we boast of "our good *deeds*." We humbly confess "our *offences*." Christ is the only "Ark" of safety, outside of which billow the "roaring waters of divine wrath." Only when we are under Christ's protection shall we enter the Kingdom of heaven.[32] Conversion and holiness are gifts of the Holy Spirit. Good works play "*no part whatever* in our acceptance and justification with God." Once liberated from the yoke of sin, however, the sinner should perform good works out of gratitude to Jesus Christ who, alone, has "freely justified him."[33]

As an Evangelical, Newman was "inclined" to make regeneration "synonymous" with conversion because, just as the eucharist is a "*sign and symbol*" of the atonement, baptism is a "*sign and symbol*" of conversion.[34] Neither atonement nor conversion takes place within either sacrament. What sacraments "*typify* is one thing, what they convey is another." Real conversion brings about a permanent change of heart. Baptism does not. Conversion conveys "certain privileges," such as the promise of paradise, and is "conditional" upon a change of heart and "generally attended by reflection, meditation and reading of Scripture under the influence of the Holy Spirit." This process takes time and cannot simply be a matter of receiving a sacrament.[35] Baptism admits a person into the visible Church as a nominal Christian. That is all. The invisible Church is reserved only for those who have experienced the saving power of Jesus Christ though the Holy Spirit.[36]

In 1825 Newman was drawn into an argument about revelation with his brother Charles, who suddenly announced that, "after a great deal of preparatory thought," he was abandoning Christianity in favour of the more rational principles of the reformer Robert Owen, who, for all practical purposes, "beats St. Paul hollow." Paul's ideas are "very ingenious," but irrelevant. From first to last, Christianity is a pack of lies and all Christians a "pack of fools" for believing such nonsense. The Bible is filled with "error and evil and meanness and folly." Christianity does not make people good. It is the other way round. Organized religion brings "evil most abundantly into the world."[37] Get rid of religion and you get rid of evil.

Charles was an emotionally unstable character.[38] The staccato rhythm of his letters at the time reflects his inner restlessness or, as he himself described it, "mental itch":

> I might say a great deal on this subject [revelation] if I were not fidgetty [*sic*]; yet, notwithstanding, I am very fidgetty, when I can manage to call up two or three ideas in my mind, I can make a very just deduction: and when I recover, as I expect in time, it will be a great pleasure to me to establish truth wherever it exists—(and I know in what quarter it lies— it does not come from the east:)—on the ruins of falsehood wherever it exists. Knowledge, knowledge is what is wanted. There is a science which has never been cultivated:—its first principles have not been observed. All the sorrow that is in the world is unnecessary; it is to be laughed at as much as deplored, and may be remedied by knowledge.[39]

In response to this "most painful" and "heart-rending" announcement, Newman drew up his first defence of Christian revelation. Charles adamantly maintained that it was perfectly legitimate to use the contents of revelation to judge its authenticity.[40] Just as adamantly, Newman insisted that revelation cannot be judged solely by content. Any rejection of Christianity originates from a "fault of the *heart*, not of the *intellect*." It is not even the result of faulty reasoning. It is about "pride" and "sensuality," which are beyond the "reach" of reason. There is no contradiction in saying "*both* that the Christian evidences are most convincing, *and yet* that they are not likely to convince those who reject them." Although the "most powerful arguments" will not "*convince*" opponents of revealed truth, they can generally "*silence*" them. The evidence for revelation may not be "*overpowering*," but it is "*unanswerable*."[41] The idea "that unassisted reason is competent to discover moral and revealed truth" is gratuitous. Revealed truth must be approached in a positive frame of mind. Not only should people feel the need for it, they have to trust God. Only then will they "possess real knowledge and true peace."[42]

The very idea of revelation implies the "revelation of something" beyond reason whose genuineness is sanctioned by its credentials and not by its contents. If content is the only criterion, then authentic revelation would be virtually impossible. Revelation stands or falls by its credentials and not by the "practice of measuring" its contents by "any preconceived ideas or morals or philosophy."[43]

It is absurd to dismiss out of hand any system, religious or secular, by "a priori" objections to its doctrines, while ignoring that "great body of external evidence" underpinning it. That is the equivalent of rejecting Newtonian physics by "expatiating on the antecedent absurdity" of anyone who thought that the earth revolved round the sun and by stubbornly refusing to look at the overwhelming external evidence in its favour. There is not one set of rules for secular subjects and another for religious matters. They both have the same set of "purely logical principles," and revelation is subject to the same rigorous principles and scrutiny by which all truth is judged.[44] Yet when some people talk about revelation, they have no scruple in reversing the "legitimate process of reasoning." If they criticized a Newton or a Lavoisier in a similar fashion, they would be guilty of "unfair" play.[45]

Before his last letter to Charles on the subject, Newman announced a series of sermons on revelation, to commence immediately. In making the announcement, he reminded his parishioners about the "immense importance of holiness, as the very end and purpose of all revelation."[46] The aim of the gospel is to restore Christians to the purity of Adam before the Fall, to make "religion practicable, possible, delightful," and to "infuse into it that humility which becomes the fallen condition." After which comes faith in the atonement followed by gratitude and love. Finally, the gospel's aim is to teach dependence on the Holy Spirit "which our feebleness makes indispensable."[47]

This reminder about holiness was no more than a lengthy quote borrowed from an introductory essay by Daniel Wilson for an edition of Butler's *Analogy of Religion* which Newman had just read.[48] As an Evangelical, Wilson was critical of Butler's "limited" presentation of his argument. It may have been "clear and convincing" for an educated person, but he felt that "the young reader," particularly the "inexperienced theological student," would find his style "too close, too negligent, too obscure." Butler's statements about Christianity were "somewhat restricted" and impersonal. "The full and exuberant grace and consolation of Christianity in its particular doctrines, and its application to the heart and life were not indeed the topics of our great author."[49]

Admittedly, Butler had "nobly defended" the "commanding truths" of revelation. His "powerful argument" was excellent as far as it went, but it did not go far enough. There was very little mention of "practical religion" or references to the great Evangelical doctrines such as "the precise nature of our justification before God," "the extent of the fall and ruin of man by sin," the "work of the Holy Spirit in regeneration and sanctification," the "consolatory, cheering, vivifying effects of conscience," "communion with

God," or "hope of rest and joy in heaven." If Butler had done that, the "inexperienced theological student" would have been rescued from the "danger of drawing erroneous conclusions, on some practical points of great importance."[50]

For example, misunderstandings have arisen, from time to time, about the meaning of natural religion as defined by Butler and its "efficacy, independently of Christianity." People either deny its existence or put it on a par with revealed religion. While natural religion was "originally impressed" on the heart of every person, that imprint was completely "effaced by the fall," after which all those "habits and acts of subjection, obedience, reverence, love, adoration, gratitude, trust, prayer, communion, resignation, and praise" could be restored only by the "light and grace of Christianity." Without it, natural religion remains "impotent and helpless," and the human race stumbles from bad to worse. "No example has ever been produced," Wilson claimed, "either of a pagan nation acting up to the scattered notices of religion which it possessed, or recovering the purity of it when once lost by the lapse of time, or the progress of vice." Any surviving "relics of truth" are in themselves "impotent" and simply reinforce "in every age, and in every quarter of the world, the indispensable necessity and infinite importance of Christianity."[51]

At the time Newman seems to have been as much, if not more, influenced by Wilson's essay as he was by Butler's argument. Wilson and Butler disagreed on the link between natural and revealed religion, the latter maintaining that the natural world was a reflection of the supernatural world, and Wilson disagreeing. Thus, a dilemma for Newman, in which he opted generally for Wilson but leant occasionally towards Butler. The sermons also reveal the influence of Thomas Erskine and the idea of revelation as "manifestation" or message. That is, revelation is a system intended to reveal God "completely."[52] As we shall see, this was a position he was later to reject.[53]

The sermons themselves present revelation as a crystal-clear system of haves versus have-nots, of light versus darkness. The world of light belongs to the Jewish and Christian dispensations—the only two, but not co-equal partners in God's "grand general scheme of revelation" beginning with Adam.[54] Beyond the world of light lies the darkness of the heathen world devoid of any revelation whatsoever. Even its wisest philosophers lived in almost total ignorance of the "first principles" of morality. Most of them looked down on love and humility as human weakness.[55] Aristotle, Zeno, and Pythagoras, who were not without some moral principles, probably did not, but the majority did.[56]

There are two classes of revelation—those that are common to Judaism and Christianity equally and exclusively—and those that belong to Christianity exclusively. Judaism and Christianity share six common doctrines. The first is the "existence of one and only one God." The second "distinguishing doctrine" that any "heathen hardly acknowledged" was the providence of that God who "works in and by every thing, wisely, judiciously, and well." The third one is that revelation alone discloses a "moral system, a code of laws sanctioned by rewards and punishments" and founded on the "authority of an Almighty Lawgiver." The fourth tells us that God is "all-knowing, all-wise, good, merciful, true, just and holy," and that God alone is the "substance of all revelation from the time of Adam." Newman again toys with the possibility that one or two heathens "may occasionally have hinted at" some of these attributes, but, "as a whole" and as a "system of doctrines," only Jewish and Christian knowledge of these truths can "fairly be included in the light which revelation has poured upon the world." The characteristic of every authentic revelation recorded in scripture is that God's character "is held up as a *pattern to us*."[57] The fifth doctrine is the Fall and subsequent corruption of the human race. The sixth doctrine is God's promise of "restoration and recovery."[58] Because these last two doctrines prefigure Jesus Christ, who was to be the climax of revelation, they hold pride of place.[59]

Theoretically, these doctrines are discoverable by reason without the need for a direct revelation, provided a person searches for them in the right frame of mind.[60] The wisest heathens, however, were ignorant of the "first principles of religion" because they were unable to look at the world from a religious point of view. One or two of them may have had some idea of God but, because their minds were "cramped and shackled" by sin, they could not see the "seeds of truth" scattered in the "waste wilderness." Any *a priori* knowledge of God was the work of "an evil conscience" within. Even with the "book of nature" open in front of him, no heathen could ever "read fluently the doctrines of Providence and virtue."[61]

Then, there are five additional doctrines that belong exclusively to Christianity. Unlike the common six, these are beyond human reason, which is why we call them "revealed" doctrines. Yet, once revealed, they become self-evident principles. God revealed them "little by little, here and there," until, finally, "all five became visible."[62] They focus on the person of Jesus Christ who rescued us from darkness and the shackles of sin. "Thus there are altogether *five* evangelical doctrines—first the *atonement* which is the foundation of all and then depending on it, eternal punishment the desert of sin, pardon on repentance, grace to sanctify, and the prospect of heaven and of a resurrection of the body."[63]

The "fundamental principle" of the revealed system is Christ's atonement, which is the "only warrantable foundation" on which anyone has hope of eternal happiness.[64] On this one doctrine, the other four depend. There is "no good reason" for supposing that it was known in all its full splendour to the ancient Jews. God delayed it until the people of Israel had experienced the incontrovertible fact of human corruption. Had it been disclosed prematurely, its great message would have got lost. Thus, Christ's atonement appeals profoundly and reasonably to humanity's experience of the need for one.[65]

The people of Israel had no idea of the Messiah's identity. Their only guiding light was God's promise of a deliverer who would eventually vanquish evil and establish a Kingdom. Scripture spoke of conflict and suffering as a prelude to victory. Yet, as to his actual identity, God remained tight-lipped. Although there was nothing to guarantee certainty, there was everything to hope for.[66] Such was the Jewish dispensation.

While many parts of the gospel message are beyond human reason, there is much that is "agreeable" to it. Revealed truth demonstrates that the "God of nature" and scripture are one and the same. Admittedly, no one could possibly learn from nature that God's Son would eventually be the long-awaited Messiah. Yet, once revealed, the mediatorial office of Christ seemed to dove-tail neatly into the natural "plan of things," where the rich mediate for the poor, the learned for the ignorant, the strong for the weak, the old for the young, the innocent for the guilty, and the just for the unjust. If this is mystery in nature, Christ's atonement is even more "incomprehensible and mysterious" in supernature.[67]

Although immature and derivative, the 1825 revelation sermons are still a starting point in any investigation of Newman on revelation because they show the theological leap he was about to take.

Notes

1. *Apo.*, p. 1.

2. *G.A.*, p. 56. On the inside cover of a small Bible given to him by his father in 1807, Newman wrote that he "used no Bible so much as this."

3. BOA Letter to Aunt Elizabeth, 25 July 1844.

4. *Apo.*, p. 1.

5. *Ibid.*, p. 3. Newman kept a copy of Paine's *Age of Reason, Part the Third* in his room at the Birmingham Oratory (BOA A. 8. 5.). Tom Mozley, a student of Newman's at Oriel College, recalled that Newman "had Tom Paine's works under lock and key, and lent them with much caution to such as could bear the shock" (*Reminiscences Chiefly of Oriel College and the Oxford Movement*, I, 40).

6. *Ibid.*, p. 4.

7. *A.W.*, p. 268.

8. *Apo.*, pp. 4-5.

9. *Ibid.*, p. 7. There is no unanimity on whether Newman's conversion resulted in his becoming an Evangelical. C. S. Dessain and J. E. Linnan represent opposing views. Dessain argues that the experience succeeded in converting him to the spiritual life, but not in any special Evangelical way. Linnan, on the other hand, argues that it was an Evangelical conversion and that Newman's documents at the time and his strict code of conduct in his early days at Oxford were recognizably Evangelical. Considering that Mayers himself was an Evangelical and the "human means" that God used for his conversion, together with the Calvinistic contents of the books he read at the time, the doctrines he espoused, and that the conversion conformed to the Evangelical norms of the day, Linnan concludes that it could not have been anything but Evangelical. See C. S. Dessain, "Newman's First Conversion," *Newman Studien* 3, pp. 37-53; J. E. Linnan, *The Evangelical Background of John Henry Newman: 1816-1826*, Vol. II, pp. 311-46.

10. G. Best, "Evangelicalism and the Victorians," *The Victorian Crisis of Faith*, A. Symondson (ed.), pp. 40-4.

11. *Ibid.*, p. 39.

12. Evangelicalism focussed on the atonement and "Christus Redemptor" (Christ the Redeemer), while Anglicanism did on the Incarnation and "Christus Consummator" (Christ who brings all things to perfection). See Y. Brilioth, *The Anglican Revival*, p. 41; V. F. Storr, *The Development of English Theology in the Nineteenth Century: 1800-1860*, pp. 73-4.

13. G. R. Balleine, *A History of the Evangelical Party in the Church of England*, p. 135.

14. G. F. A. Best, "Evangelicals and the Established Church," *Journal of Theological Studies*, N.S., Vol. X, Part 1, April 1959, p. 65.

15. J. E. Linnan, *The Evangelical Background of John Henry Newman: 1816-1826*, Vol. I, pp. 214-5. At the time, rejection of baptismal regeneration had become the "touchstone of Evangelical orthodoxy" (T. L. Sheridan, *Newman on Justification*, p. 23).

16. G. F. A. Best, *op. cit.*, pp. 68-9.

17. J. E. Linnan,., Vol. I, p. 214.

18. *Apo.*, p. 5.

19. T. Scott, *The Theological Works of the Rev. Thomas Scott* (Edinburgh, 1841), pp. 340-1.

20. T. Scott, *Essays on the Most Important Subjects in Religion* (ninth edition, London, 1822), p. 14.

21. *Ibid.*, pp. 15-7.

22. *Ibid.*, pp. 202; 205-6; 207-8.

23. *Ibid.*, p. 17.

24. *A.S.* I., 310.

25. *Apo.*, p. 6; W. Law, *A Serious Call to a Devout and Holy Life: Adapted to the State and Condition of All Orders of Christians* (a new edition, London, 1824), p. 263.

26. *A.W.*, p. 181.

27. C. Simeon, *Helps to Composition: or, Six Hundred Skeletons of Sermons*, Vol. IV (third edition, London, 1815), pp. 299-303.

28. These include: 1. "On the Necessity of a thorough reception of the doctrines contained in the 9th Article and the first part of the 10th" (May 1821); 2. "Comment on Phil. 2. xii and xiii" (June 1821); 3. "A Collection of Scripture passages setting forth in due order of succession the doctrines of Christianity (June 1821); 4. "Papers on Conversion" (June, July 1821); 5. "The Nature of Holiness" (1822 or 1823?).

29. BOA A. 9. 1. "On the Necessity of a thorough reception of the doctrines contained in the

9th Article and the first part of the 10th" (May 1821).

30. BOA A. 9. 1. "Papers on Conversion" (June, July 1821).

31. *Ibid.*

32. *A.S.* I, 327.

33. BOA A. 17. 1., Sermon 61 (6 Mar. 1825), "justification through faith only," p. 12.

34. In March, 1825, Newman made some notes for a local clerical meeting "on treating baptized persons as regenerate." He wrote: "I have long considered it [baptismal regeneration] the burning point" (BOA A. 7. 1.).

35. BOA A. 9. 1., "The Nature of Holiness."

36. BOA A. 50. 2., Sermon 121 (4 Dec. 1825), "on the use of the visible Church," pp. 3-4; 6-7; 13.

37. BOA A. 4. 2. The Charles Correspondence is preserved in BOA. Various members of the Newman family transcribed both Charles' letters and Newman's replies into eight exercise books.

38. *L.D.* I, pp. 182-3.

39. BOA A. 4. 2.

40. *L.D.* I, pp. 240.

41. *Ibid.*, p. 246.

42. *Ibid.*, p. 228.

43. *Ibid.*, pp. 240; 226.

44. *Ibid.*, p. 214.

45. *Ibid.*, p. 219.

46. BOA A. 17. 1., Sermon 103 (4 Sept. 1825), "holiness, the end of the Gospel," p. 14.

47. *Ibid.*, pp. 10-1.

48. J. Butler, *The Analogy of Religion, Natural and Revealed, to the Constitution and Course of Nature*, ed. Daniel Wilson (Glasgow, 1824), pp. cxiii-cxiv. Wilson's essay is 161 pages long.

49. *Ibid.*, pp. x-xi; cvi.

50. *Ibid.*, pp. civ-cvi.

51. *Ibid.*, pp. cviii-cxi.

52. In the final sermon of the series, Newman acknowledges Erskine as the source of his ideas on the atonement (A.S. II., pp. 384-5). He paraphrases some of his ideas:

> If the object our Maker had in view had been merely to pardon us, there would have been no need of revealing to us the sacrifice of Christ [Erskine]. But He might have pardoned us without our knowing it before we came into another world. But if (as is the case) His object was to regenerate and sanctify our hearts,—to convert us from sin and make us love Him—for this a display of His character was necessary—and a display of Himself in action—and a display not only of His holiness, justice and truth, but also of His love—in order, through His grace, to warm our hearts and fix them upon Him, weaning us from evil and winning us over to the truth (*Ibid.*, pp. 385-6).

See T. Erskine, *Remarks on the Internal Evidences for the Truth of Revealed Religion*, pp. 71ff.

53. See Chapter 9, "Revelation and Mystery," pp. 123-32.

54. BOA A. 17. 1., Sermon 110 (16 Oct. 1825), "feelings produced in common by all revelation" (2), p. 2.

55. BOA A. 17. 1., Sermon 108 (5 Sept. 1825), "on the principles common to all revelations," pp. 1- 2.

56. BOA A. 17. 1., Sermon 106 (18 Sept. 1825), "state of the heathen world etc.," pp. 9-12. See *A.W.*, p. 82; *L.D.* II, 281; BOA A. 7. 1.

57. BOA Sermon 108, pp. 4-8.

58. *Ibid.*, pp. 8-11.

59. *Ibid.*, pp. 11; 16.
60. *A.S.* II, 374.
61. *Ibid.*, p. 379; BOA Sermon 108, p. 18.
62. *Ibid.*, pp 373-4.
63. *Ibid.*, p. 354.
64. *Ibid.*, p. 367.
65. *Ibid.*, pp. 354ff.
66. *Ibid.*, pp. 355-6.
67. *Ibid.*, pp. 381ff.

CHAPTER 2

Years of Transition

Giving a progress report on his first three weeks at St Clement's, Newman, ordained deacon in June 1824, exudes the confidence of a young Evangelical bringing "a new broom."[1] He had already picked up that some parishioners were finding his teaching on the atonement "unpalatable." Nevertheless, he was not going to compromise because the "doctrine of Christ crucified is the only spring of real virtue and piety, and the only foundation of peace and comfort." Like Thomas Scott, he was convinced that truth, however unpalatable, would ultimately win the day.[2] By contrast, a later letter to his sister indicates that he had begun to change. While pleased that Harriett liked his sermons, he cautioned her against taking his opinions on "trust" too quickly. He had already changed his mind on several matters and would probably do so again. "I see I know very little about any thing, though I often think I know a great deal."[3] In the meantime, his theological views had come under fire from Whately, Lloyd, and Hawkins, whose opinions he respected. Working in a poor parish convinced him that Evangelicalism, as he had preached and practised it, did not reflect the way ordinary Christians live.

Earlier on, Richard Whately had taken a painfully shy Newman under his wing, tested his intellectual fibre, trained him to "think correctly," and instilled much-needed self-confidence.[4] He came round to Whately's idea of a divinely appointed visible Church in which people were admitted to full membership through baptism, which was endowed with unique rights and privileges and was independent of the State.[5] By this stage, he was now talking about "that visible Christian body and society instituted by Christ and His Apostles professing the one faith of the gospel, governed by certain officers, and associated by certain laws, however the members of it may be divided by difference of country, language, manners or civilization."[6] It was the only "place of grace, of strength, of renewal, of conversion, of salvation." Without it, there is "no revealed way." Christians who do not "habitually frequent" it have no real reason for thinking that "they are members of Christ or inheritors of His future glory."[7]

If Whately taught Newman to think logically and critically, Charles

Lloyd, Regius Professor of Divinity, helped him to theologize methodically. In addition to attending an "annual set of public lectures," which was compulsory for students seeking ordination, Newman also attended a series of private lectures between October 1823 and February 1826.[8] Instead of concentrating on "dogma or philosophy," these lectures focussed on "exegetical criticism, historical research, and controversy." Lloyd was more interested in the "grounds of Christian faith than on the faith itself." When it came to revealed religion, he preferred external evidences (proofs) to internal ones.[9] Apart from asking questions, he encouraged students to talk, but demanded "direct, full, and minutely accurate answers."[10]

Edward Hawkins criticized the severity of Newman's first sermon for its implied rejection of baptismal regeneration.[11] Hawkins took exception to Newman's arbitrary division of Christians into converted and unconverted. No such "line of demarcation" existed. No one has the right to make such an artificial distinction. People may not be as good as they could be, but they were certainly better than they might be. Differences in "religious and moral excellence" are matters of degree. Hawkins offered him J. B. Sumner's *Apostolical Preaching* to read.[12] Newman resolved to approach it with an open mind. In fact, if he could find "any mention of grace being irrespectively connected with baptism, I have every reason for catching at it." Beyond "any thing else," *Apostolical Preaching* succeeded in "routing out evangelical doctrines" from his creed and convinced him, once and for all, about the validity of baptismal regeneration.[13] Hawkins' views of tradition also made a lasting impression. Until then, Newman saw scripture as the sole, infallible teacher of the revealed word of God. But, tradition also played an important role in determining it. He was of the opinion "that the sacred text was never intended to teach doctrine, but only to prove it, and that, if we would learn doctrine, we must have recourse to the formularies of the Church" such as the "Catechism" and "Creeds."[14] Teaching tradition is the Church's responsibility. Verifying it is scripture's.

In the early days of their friendship, Edward Bouverie Pusey presented Newman with the paradox of someone who seemed liberal, lived like an Evangelical, but did not hesitate to criticize the Evangelical rejection of baptismal regeneration.[15] Pusey respected the idea of a Christian sabbath, loved scripture and displayed personal holiness, all of which seemed to indicate the presence of the Holy Spirit.[16]

Newman's "great change in his religious opinions" happened in the middle of twenty months of "hard parish work."[17] Going about his duties, he met parishioners not of the classic Evangelical mould but not without sanctifying grace. Evidence seemed to be saying that "Calvinism was not a key to the phenomena of human nature, as they occur in the world."[18] Even before leaving St Clement's, he told parishioners that the doctrine of election should not be a "source of anxiety and perplexity." Since scripture said nothing definite one way or the other, and since it was too difficult "for our own feeble reason" to fathom, he was urging them to stop agonizing and stop jumping to hasty conclusions, but to trust God who wants *"all men"* to be saved."[19] Let us "safely leave the matter to God," because it is God's business, not ours.[20] In moving away from Evangelicalism, Newman later saw himself drifting to liberalism.[21] Some people have since thought this an exaggeration. The truth is that Newman did dally with liberalism for a time, as some sermons of the period show.[22] Indeed, he retrospectively tagged some of them as "Whatelyan."[23] In one sermon he suggests that Christian liberty "consists in our knowing in great measure the *reasons* of the divine commands and having strong motives for complying with them, in other words in opposition to a blind obedience"; that, in the gospel, "Christ has supplied us with *principles* which act as *foundations* for a large and enlightened *knowledge* of our duty, as *sanctions* for *enforcing* it upon us, and as *motives* for our *performing* it."[24] In another sermon he says that the Trinity "is not one doctrine, but a *set of doctrines*, collected together and viewed in a particular light by the Church"; that "it is scriptural facts reduced to order by man"; that "our rational belief in it becomes a test of our having examined it carefully and humbly"; and that " it seems intended to teach us that our belief in it must be *practical*, not merely intellectual and abstract."[25]

Reading the early Church Fathers for the first time proved unsatisfactory because, on Lloyd's advice, he read them chronologically, starting with Ignatius and Justin Martyr.[26] Some "shreds and tatters" of Evangelicalism still coloured his reading.[27] Apart from gaining insight into the "prerogatives" and "gifts of the Episcopate," it was a waste of time. On reflection, he had been searching the text for what it had to say on justification, faith, holiness, and so on. Looking for what was not there, he "missed what was there."[28] At the time, he criticized Justin for being "almost silent" on the atonement and for knowing "mighty little" about St Paul, and was annoyed to find "no definite allusion to the doctrine of the Holy Spirit's renovating *influences*."[29]

He later suggested that anyone reading the Fathers should have some prior knowledge of theology and church history before launching into them, and that it was "best to get a footing" in a "particular controversy."[30] Above all, the reader had to keep an open mind:

Whatever then be the true way of interpreting the Fathers, and in particular the Apostolical Fathers, if a man begins by summoning them before him, instead of betaking himself to them,—by seeking to make them evidence for modern dogmas, instead of throwing his mind upon their text, and drawing from them their own doctrines,—he will to a certainty miss their sense.[31]

In the following years, his understanding of the Church deepened. The Evangelical distinction between a "visible and invisible" body became "irrelevant" and "unscriptural." It simply does not matter "whether we say it is to the visible or invisible body that pardon and grace are given and final perseverance promised, for they are one and the same."[32] As members of Christ's mystical body, Christians "ought to live together in a visible society here on earth, not as a confused unconnected multitude, but united and organised one with another, by an established order, so as evidently to appear and to act as one."[33] The Church "does not depend on individual Christians, but is before them in honour and in age."[34]

Not only are Baptism and the Eucharist the "general and ordinary means of salvation," they are the "only ordained authorized means of conveying it."[35] They form the heart of the liturgy. United worship is not just "a means of grace," it is "the very chief means."[36] By their social nature, sacraments demand that they be performed in public:

> They cannot be celebrated except Christians meet in a body—Since then the ordinances which especially convey grace are committed to the Church or body of Christians as assembled together, we cannot gain grace without seeking it from the body [Church]—i.e. we cannot be independent—we cannot stand by ourselves apart from others—we dare not separate from our brethren and set up assemblies for ourselves—we must take the blessing home to us from Church, because we cannot gain it in the first instance simply in our private room, because the Sacraments which convey the blessing are performed in Church.[37]

God's grace was promised primarily "through the Sacraments, and through whatever has a sacramental character," such as "public prayer," which carries more weight than a sermon.[38] As far back as apostolical times, obedience to church authority was essential for the "preservation of the faith, purity of doctrine, the quiet growth of piety in private Christians, and precision and clearness in the general operations of the Church."[39] Therefore, any "divisions" or "dissent" must be "severely censored," because the only reliable guide in religious matters is the "great antiquity and consistent testimony of Christ's Church."[40] Bishops are the "protectors against schism" and, through the priesthood, sacraments are administered.[41] In the performance of sacerdotal duties, no priest has the right to speak as a private citizen. His primary duty

> . . . is to be a teacher of others—to save, not only himself, but them that hear him. Of him is required a systematic knowledge of doctrine, an insight into the analogy of faith, and a penetrating foresight of the distant and ultimate consequences and slight incipient deflections from the truth. He is intended to be, from his office, the guide of those who in many cases cannot adequately enter into the grounds of his advice. The Christian minister is the appointed and ordinary centre of knowledge and reliance, in all religious and moral points.[42]

At about the same time, Newman's understanding of revelation was being transformed by the Butlerian perception of personal conscience and Justin's concept of the *Logos spermatikos*. Clement's contribution was to come later.

By now, he had begun to accept that everyone, including heathens, had a personal conscience from which they could extract such "broad natural principles" as the "knowledge of a Creator and Governor of the world, and of the general duty of virtue."[43] If we follow these principles faithfully, there is "no limit to the power of natural conscience" in teaching individuals their moral duty, independently of revelation, Jewish or Christian.[44] Whatever we do, we must "obey" our conscience "rigidly," because to act otherwise is "a great sin." Christ "did not come primarily to teach us" our moral duties, "for this plain reason:—*because we might have known them without His informing us*, whereas a revelation implies something which we could not have known without Him." He came to "*die for our sins*." All other moral truths had already been discovered by "natural reason and conscience." In fact, there is probably not a "single precept" in the New Testament that had not already been "laid down by heathen moralists who never saw the Scriptures."[45]

Shortly afterwards, Newman read Justin Martyr. It is then that he seems to have made the connection between "broad natural principles" derived from conscience, and divine revelation which reaches its perfection in Christ. God had indeed revealed aspects of the Godhead in the Old and New Testaments. But God had also revealed certain aspects through the personal conscience of every person, in every age, from time immemorial.

A definite "parallel" exists between the "mediatorial plan of salvation" as revealed in scripture and in the day-to-day affairs of this world. In revealing Jesus Christ to the world, God did not suddenly invent a new "mode of acting" for the Incarnation. God adopted the same system already at work "everywhere and in every age for the preservation and benefit of the human race." This system of blessing humanity through the "mediation of others" is called God's "Providence," the whole of which is carried on within a "system of continual mediation." Parents are the "instruments of God's bounties to their children." Food, clothing, housing, medicine "are all gifts from Providence—but none come immediately from Him." Everything is mediated through the "instrumentality of others."[46]

The parallel between the "revealed system" and "visible Providence, the system of grace and the system of nature, shows that they are appointments of one and the same being, working at sundry times and in diverse manners, but on consistent principles." The God of Jesus Christ "shows Himself by His revealed works to be the God of that course of worldly affairs, which we see" everywhere, every day. Such a parallel is "no slight confirmation to us of the divine authority of Scripture doctrine."[47] Before the "system of divine mediation" had been "openly and authoritatively announced" in Christ, "it had already been traced out," not only among the Jews, but also among the "heathen philosophers themselves":

> Our blessed Saviour came to build up and put in order the house of God which men's sins since the fall have broken to pieces. He was not content to reveal religious truths and let them take their chance course—to send down His gift of grace to dwell unknown in the world, as in former ages—He lodged His gifts in a home where men might go for them and be sure to find—He collected together the remnants of those former revelations by which men know their duty and put them into form; he confirmed them and added to them. Before He came, truth had for the most part been in pilgrimage.[48]

The essence of all true religion is faith, which is the "food and strength of every good man in every age."[49] When Aristotle says:

> "I will follow moral excellence without reference to the pleasure which may or may not attend it, because it is good and my best instincts prompt me to follow it," he is but acting the part of Abraham who took God as his portion without definite promise. In both is the same self neglect and self denial, and resolute and noble disinterestedness in trusting to the voice of God without reference to present enjoyment.[50]

Even though many "an ungifted heathen," such as Rahab, Namaan, and Cornelius may have had "less light," they are often "better men and holier than those who have much light." On the day of general judgment, they will probably "shame us Christians with their one talent."[51]

Notes

1. *L.D.* I, 196.

2. *Ibid.*, 180-1.

3. *Ibid.*, 280.

4. *L.D.* XV, 176-7; *A.W.*, p. 68.

5. *A.W.*, p. 69; *Apo.*, p. 12.

6. BOA A. 50. 1., Sermon 157 (19 Nov. 1826), "On the One Catholic and Apostolic Church," p. 2.

7. A.S. I, p. 185.

8. *A.W.*, p. 70. See "John Henry Newman and Dr Charles Lloyd," Donald A. Withey, *Downside Review* (Oct. 1993), pp. 235-50.

9. [E. S. Ffoulkes], *A History of the Church of S. Mary the Virgin Oxford, by the present Vicar* (London, 1892), p. 404.

10. *A.W.*, pp. 70-1.

11. BOA A. 50. 6; Sermon 2, "Waiting on God." Preached while still a deacon on 23 June 1824 at Over Worton, near Woodstock. The doctrine of baptismal regeneration was the burning theological issue of the day.

12. *Apostolical Preaching* (London, 1839, eighth edition), p. iv. John Bird Sumner (1780-1862), a middle-of-the-road Evangelical, was an advocate of baptismal regeneration and a critic of the high moral tone of Calvinism in some sections of the Church of England. He became bishop of Chester in 1828 and archbishop of Canterbury in 1848. He wrote *Apostolical Preaching* in 1815.

13. BOA A. 3. 4; see *A.W.*, pp. 77-8; *Diff.* I, 25n.

14. *Apo.*, p. 9.

15. *A.W.*, p. 203. See L. Frappell, "The Early Intellectual Development of E. B. Pusey," in *Pusey Rediscovered*, ed. P. Butler. Newman was elected a fellow of Oriel College on 12 April 1822. Pusey was elected a fellow on 4 April 1823 and appointed Regius (Crown) Professor of Hebrew on 14 Nov. 1828.

16. *Ibid.*, pp. 75-6.

17. *Ibid.*, pp. 72-3.

18. *Ibid.*, pp. 206; 79.

19. BOA A. 17. 1., Sermon 150, "general observations on the subject. conclusion," pp. 14-5. Farewell sermon at St Clement's, 23 April 1825.

20. *A.S* II, 345.

21. *Apo.*, pp. 13-4.

22. A. J. Boekraad is incorrect in arguing that Newman's anti-liberalism is evident even in his early writing. See A. J. Boekraad, *The Personal Conquest of Truth*, p. 97. 23. Among the authors he was consulting throughout this period was the Dutch Arminian, Hugo Grotius (1583-1645), and the German biblical scholar, Ernst Rosenmüller (1768-1835). About this time also, Pusey, who was studying with Johann Eichhorn (1752-1827) at Göttingen and Friedrich Schleiermacher (1768-1834) in Berlin, was warning Newman against the "rationalizing implication of distinguishing apostolic from post-apostolic miracles" (BOA, Sermon 104, Appendix, re-preached 11 June 1826; Frappell, *op. cit.*, pp. 9; 31.).

24. BOA A. 50. 1., 2 Sept. 1827, "On the Christian law of liberty," pp. 4; 4a; 13-4.

25. BOA A.50. 1. (1 June 1828), "On the doctrine of the Trinity," pp. 5; 21.

26. *Apo.*, p. 25; *K.C.* p. 197.

27. *A.W.*, p. 78.

28. *Diff.* I, 371; *K.C.*, p. 196.

29. BOA D. 18. 1. "The Theological Commonplace Book," columns 21; 23; 24.

30. *K.C.*, pp. 196-7.

31. *Ess.* I, 228.

32. BOA A. 9. 1., "Remarks on the Covenant of Grace," 1828.

33. *P.S.* VII, 234.

34. *A.S.* I, 12.

35. *Ibid.*, p. 13.

36. *Ibid.*, p. 10.

37. *Ibid.*, p. 13.

38. *Ibid.*, p. 26.

39. BOA Sermon 216 (15 Nov. 1829), "On Church—union, and the sin of schism," p. 22. See *P.S.* VII, 17.

40. *Ibid.*, pp. 17-8.

41. *Ibid.*, p. 3.

42. BOA A. 50. 2., Sermon 323 (18 Dec. 1831), "On the Ministerial Order, as an existing divine institution. Ordination Sermon," p. 8.

43. BOA A. 50. 1., Sermon 161 (2 Sept. 1827), "On the Christian law of liberty," pp. 19-20.

44. *Ibid.*, p. 11. See J. Butler, Sermon II, 19: "Had it strength, as it had right; had it power, as it has manifest authority, it would absolutely govern the world."

45. *Ibid.*, pp. 10ff.

46. *A.S.* I, 213.

47. *Ibid.*, p. 214.

48. *Ibid.*, pp. 82-3.

49. *A.S.* II, 140.

50. BOA A. 7. 1. (August 1829).

51. *A.S.* II, 189.

CHAPTER 3

Justin Martyr, Clement of Alexandria, Bishop Butler

Paramount among the Church Fathers Newman was reading at this time were Justin Martyr and Clement of Alexandria, whose catechetical aim was to present the Christian message to a largely Hellenistic world as "intellectually respectable," and to define it in terms of that culture.[1] They needed to evaluate the significance of pagan philosophies for Christianity, to establish a viable link between Greek philosophy and Christian revelation, and to establish some status for a Plato or a Homer within the system. It was this "broad philosophy" of Justin and Clement which so fired Newman's imagination:

> Some portions of their teaching, magnificent in themselves, came like music to my inward ear, as if the response to ideas, which, with little external to encourage them, I had cherished so long. They were based on the mystical or sacramental principle, and spoke of the various Economies or Dispensations of the Eternal. I understood these passages to mean that the exterior world, physical and historical, was but the manifestation to our senses of realities greater than itself. Nature was a parable: Scripture was an allegory: pagan literature, philosophy, and mythology, properly understood, were but a preparation for the Gospel. The Greek poets and sages were in a certain sense prophets; for "thoughts beyond their thought to those high bards were given." There had been a directly divine dispensation granted to the Jews; but there had been in some sense a dispensation carried on in favour of the Gentiles. He who had taken the seed of Jacob for His elect people had not therefore cast the rest of mankind out of His sight.[2]

In the Johannine tradition, Justin believed that the divine Logos had implanted into every age, race, and individual seeds of divine truth, which he called the *Logos spermatikos*. God's purpose was to lead everyone everywhere to some knowledge of the truth, however obscure and fragmentary.[3] In a special way, the divine Logos, who is Jesus Christ, had

45

implanted seeds of divine truth in the hearts and minds of the Greeks, thus enabling them to "participate in the life of the Logos," even though the knowledge gained was also shadowy and fragmented.[4] Justin was not out to make a systematic attempt at synthesis between Hellenism and Christianity. "It was simply and truly a personal confession of faith in the pre-existent Christ, present and active among the Greeks, sowing the seeds of truth in their midst."[5] He stopped short of saying that these seeds were an actual preparation for the gospel. Clement of Alexandria thought that they were and said so.

Some were suspicious of pagan philosophies. These included the uncompromising Tatian and Tertullian, who branded philosophy as the "fountain of all heresies."[6] Non-Christians were equally suspicious. About the year 178, Celsus the Epicurean retaliated by arguing in his *True Logos* that Hellenism was "the most relevant expression of the cultural tradition" of humanity. By comparison, Judaism and Christianity were "bad imitations."[7] It is probable that Clement had Celsus in mind when writing the *Stromateis*.

To a greater degree than predecessors or contemporaries, Clement addressed himself to reconciling Christianity and Hellenism. Not only a Christian Platonist and a Christian humanist, he was probably the first writer of the early Church, in the literary sense of the word.[8] While Justin highlighted humanity's capacity to appropriate certain elementary truths by the light of the Logos, Clement went further by saying that Hellenism and Christianity shared a common tradition:[9]

> Never before had the early Church been told so boldly that there was good in Paganism, and that her sacred Scriptures were the highest but not the only documents which revealed the will of God. Never before in the library of a Christian man of learning had Plato and Euripides been so frankly claimed as friends. Never before had those who hesitated to come over been so encouraged to recognise the abiding value of treasures that already were their own. Inclusive, not exclusive, was the character of Clement's Christianity, and wherever he may wander in the wide field of literature, he finds unsuspected traces of the influence of the Word.[10]

In the search for truth, philosophy was a useful partner provided that it did not trespass into other areas.[11] A philosopher is like a wild olive tree

> ... in having much that is undigested, on account of his devotion to the search, his propensity to follow, and his eagerness to seize the fatness of the truth; if he get besides the divine power, through faith, by being transplanted into the good and mild knowledge, like the wild olive,

engrafted in the truly fair and merciful Word, he both assimilates the nutriment that is supplied, and becomes a fair and good olive tree. For engrafting makes worthless shoots noble, and compels the barren to be fruitful by the art of culture and by gnostic skill.[12]

Greek philosophy's real strength lay in its capacity to neutralize the "assault of sophistry" and detect "treacherous plots" hatched against truth.[13] It is the "Handmaid of Theology," a "preparation" given to the Greeks "directly and primarily, till the Lord shall call them."[14] Real philosophy is not Stoicism or Platonism or Epicureanism or Aristotelianism but an "eclectic" assortment of truths scattered throughout many philosophies.[15] One particular philosophy might possess one piece of the Logos, another philosophy another piece, and so on. The mistake was to parade one piece as the whole truth.[16]

Clement used a variety of metaphors to describe the eclectic manner in which Greek "preparatory" culture and philosophy was given by God. Sometimes, it was a shower of rain falling here and there on the "good land," "dunghill," and "houses." At other times, it was a mixture of grass, wheat, figs, and "other reckless trees" growing on tops of tombs. All are types of truth, but none possesses the "same grace" as wheat flourishing in "rich soil" or as trees in a forest. God is the sower "who from the beginning . . . sowed nutritious seeds," not just one strain of wheat or vegetable or flower or tree, but a proliferation of seeds broadcast everywhere.[17] Some Greek philosophers were divinely inspired prophets:

Besides, the thoughts of virtuous men are produced through the inspiration of God; the soul being disposed in the way it is, and the divine will being conveyed to human souls, particular divine ministers contributing to such services. For regiments of angels are distributed over the nations and cities. And, perchance, some are assigned to individuals.[18]

Among the Greeks who had "hit" on the truth by divine inspiration was the "truth-loving" Plato for whom God was the measure of everything, as well as Aristotle, the Pythagoreans, Sophocles, Euripides, and Homer, all of whom "indeed bear witness that the force of truth is not hidden."[19] In addition to Greek philosophy, there are the philosophies of the "barbarians," who were more interested in truth for its own sake than the Greeks, who were obsessed with "disputing and doubting" and seduced by "love of fame."[20] By comparison, the Greeks were children. Thus philosophy, a "thing of the highest utility,"

. . . flourished in antiquity among the barbarians, shedding its light over the nations. And afterwards it came to Greece. First in its ranks were the prophets of the Egyptians; and the Chaldeans among the Assyrians; and the Druids among the Gauls; and the Samanaeans among the Bactrians;

and the philosophers among the Celts; and the Magi of the Persians, who foretold the Saviour's birth, and came into the land of Judaea guided by a star. The Indian gymnosophists are also in the number.[21]

Butler's influence on Newman came in two waves. The first came in 1825 when he read the *Analogy* in the Wilson edition, deriving "two points," which became "underlying principles" of his teaching. The first was the "very idea of an analogy between the separate works of God," and the second was that probability is the "guide of life."[22] The second wave came in 1827, possibly with the appearance of Keble's *Christian Year*, which reinforced these principles but "recast" them in a more "creative" way. In one particular sermon, his remarks on personal conscience run parallel to Butler's own remarks in three "Sermons Upon Human Nature," indicating that he was already familiar with them. Butler's *Fifteen Sermons* were originally a response to the philosophy of Thomas Hobbes and its reduction of human behaviour to the principle of selfishness, and were also directed against Calvinism's bleak picture of human nature. Butler believed that true morality consists of living in harmony with one's true nature, the principal constituents of which are love of self, benevolence and personal conscience.[23]

Personal conscience is not just one human faculty among many. Of its very nature, it is "anterior to the Gospel, supreme over all others," and carries the stamp of its own authority.[24] To substitute another faculty or passion is a "violation" of human nature.[25] From the "very economy and constitution" of the individual, conscience alone has the right to dictate human behaviour. "Had it strength, as it has right; had it power, as it has manifest authority, it would absolutely govern the world":[26]

> And from all these things put together, nothing can be more evident, than that, exclusive of revelation, man cannot be considered as a creature left by his Maker to act at random, and live at large up to the extent of his natural power, as passion, humour, wilfulness, happen to carry him; which is the condition brute creatures are in: but that *from his make, constitution, or nature, he is in the strictest and most proper sense a law to himself.* He hath the rule of right within: what is wanting is only that he should honestly attend to it.[27]

Not only does conscience point us in the right direction, it is "our natural guide . . . assigned us by the Author of our nature." Therefore, it is our duty to "follow this guide" without looking for ways and means to circumvent it "with impunity."[28]

Thus, Justin Martyr seems to have opened up the possibility of divine revelation outside Judaism and Christianity. Butler's explanation of personal conscience suggested one of the principal channels by which God had revealed the Godhead to every person, in every age from time immemorial. Clement of Alexandria's explanation of Hellenism and Christianity as sharing a common tradition broadened his views even more.

Notes

1. J. Daniélou, *Gospel Message and Hellenistic Culture*, p. 39; H. Chadwick (trans.), *Origen: Contra Celsum*, p. ix.

2. *Apo.*, pp. 26-7. In paying tribute to the Fathers of the Church, Newman singles out Clement of Alexandria and Origen (*c.* 185-*c.* 254) for special mention. Clement was certainly instrumental in broadening his horizons on revelation in 1831, but Newman seems to have forgotten Justin Martyr (*c.* 100 -*c.* 165), who first alerted him four years earlier to the possibility of universal revelation. In this regard, Origen's influence was minimal. Compared with Clement's approach, Origen's attitude to Greek philosophy was fairly critical and uncompromising. (See *Origen: Contra Celsum*, Book VI, Sections 3-4, pp. 317-8.)

3. Justin Martyr, *First Apology*, (ANCL), 5: 10; 46: 46-7.

4. 2 *Apol.* 13: 83; 10: 79-80.

5. C. Saldanha, *Divine Pedagogy*, p. 185.

6. J. Patrick, *Clement of Alexandria*, p. 35.

7. S. R. C. Lilla, *Clement of Alexandria*, pp. 34-5.

8. C. Mondésert (ed.), *Les Stromates*: Stromate 1, Sources chrétiennes, p. 37.

9. Str. I, 1: 358.

10. R. B. Tollinton, *Clement of Alexandria* I, pp. 176-7.

11. Str. I, 20: 418.

12. Str. VI, 15: 373.

13. Str. I, 20: 420.

14. Str. I, 5: 366.

15. Str. I, 7: 374-5.

16. Str. I, 13: 389.

17. Str. I, 7: 374.

18. Str. VI, 17: 398: "For into all men whatever, especially those who are occupied with intellectual pursuits, a certain divine effluence has been instilled; wherefore, though reluctantly, they confess that God is one, indestructible, unbegotten, and that somewhere above in the tracts of heaven, in His own peculiar appropriate eminence, whence He surveys all things, He has an existence true and eternal" (Clement of Alexandria, *Exhortation to the Heathen*, ANCL, 6: 69-70; 7: 73).

19. Str. I, 8: 378; Str. V, 10: 261; *Exhortation*, 6: 69-75; 7: 73-5.

20. Str. VIII, 1: 490.

21. Str. I, 15: 398-9. According to Clement, this special inspiration was first given to the barbarian philosophers and later to the Greeks. Angels provide the last link in the "chain of philosophical tradition" in order to trace true philosophy back to God, the "fountainhead of all philosophy" (J. Danéliou, *op. cit.*, pp. 61-2).

22. *Apo.*, pp. 10-1.

23. There is some doubt as to when Newman first read Butler's *Sermons*. J. Robinson believes that Newman may have read them either "as early as the Littlemore days" in the 1840s, or in preparation for the *Grammar of Assent* in the 1860s. For the Littlemore date, he points to Newman's copy of a second-hand 1813 edition of Butler's complete works dating back to the

Littlemore days. In the front of the book, he came across a handwritten quote on Butler and conscience from one of Dr Chalmers' *Bridgewater Treatises*, which he incorrectly takes for Newman's handwriting. In fact, there is no evidence that he either bought it or read it while living there. As for the 1860s, Robinson points to an 1835 complete Butler edition which, he claims, Newman bought after 1845. Again, he mistakes the handwriting, which is indisputably that of W. H. Scott (1819-59), who bequeathed Newman his library, including that particular copy of Butler's works ("Newman's Use of Butler's Arguments," *Downside Review*, Spring 1958, Vol. 76, No. 244, pp. 175-6). See *L.D.* XIX, 274-5. 24. Sermon I, 2; Sermon II, 11.

25. Sermon II, 18. See Chapter 7, pp. 102-4.

26. Sermon II, 19.

27. Sermon III, 3.

28. Sermon III, 6. See H. Meynell, "Newman's Vindication of Faith in the *Grammar of Assent*," in I. Ker and A. G. Hill (eds.), *Newman after a Hundred Years*, pp. 247-61.

CHAPTER 4

Challenge of Liberal Anglicanism

It is difficult to find a common bond of unity between English liberals in the early part of the nineteenth century, and to differentiate them from Orthodox and Evangelicals. They were "neither intellectually nor politically monolithic," more like "members of an invisible club, the rules and purpose of which are to be inferred from private correspondences and informal associations, and not from any publicly transcribed regulations."[1] They would have disagreed with the Orthodox party for claiming that the Church of England was the "one visible, Catholic Church," and with Evangelicals about the "narrow limits within which they confined *the gospel*."[2]

In Oxford there was a group of like-minded men of liberal persuasion known as "Noetics," who, for a time, promised to become a dominant influence in the Church of England.[3] They were "possibly the last English representatives of a school of Christian apologists which had its origins in Locke's *An Essay concerning Human Understanding*."[4] They included Renn Dickson Hampden, Thomas Arnold, Baden Powell, Richard Whately, and Joseph Blanco White. Dialectic, scripture, and private judgment were their theological tools and revelation was a manifestation of truths containing practical facts deducible from history. They endorsed anti-dogmatic principles, disapproving of tradition, religious mystery, creeds, catechisms, general councils, and sacraments. Traditional explanations of the Trinity and Incarnation were human speculation based on an antiquated form of scholasticism that was "preeminently a record of the struggle" between human reason and the tyranny of authority, "civil and ecclesiastical."[5] Newman thought that they concentrated on their "enlightened views, largeness of mind, liberality of sentiment" without realizing the harm their principles were doing.[6]

The years before 1836 were significant for Newman in marking a consolidation in his understanding of the dogmatic principle. At the invitation of Hampden's predecessor, he had undertaken an edition of Dionysius of Alexandria for the University Press.[7]

This was his third serious attempt at reading the Church Fathers. His earlier treatments of "facts and Fathers" had been superficial and "*second hand*."[8] He was happier the third time round using primary sources without the aid of commentaries. The result was his being carried "forward into a very large field of reading" and learning how the early Church dealt with the Christological issues of the day.[9]

During preparatory work on Dionysius, he saw more clearly the pitfalls of rationalism and the need to respond directly and positively. The following summer, he was predicting a "flood of scepticism" to sweep the country and engulf the creed. He doubted whether local theologians had the skills to handle such a crisis. Even the "most religiously-minded" are all too quick to "give up important doctrinal truths because they do not *understand their value*." It seemed that people had learnt nothing from history. Instead of "profiting by the example of past times, we attempt to decide the most intricate questions . . . by our blind and erring reason." Scepticism had to be confronted and "smitten." That required a "single aim, a clear eye . . . a strong arm, and a courageous heart."[10] Blanco White's recent espousal of Unitarianism was a prime example of a highly intelligent person being "seduced" by rationalism.[11]

This, then, was the crucible in which Newman refined his polemical style and his thinking about revelation. It was similar to the way that the great Anglican divines of the seventeenth century had honed their ideas:

> . . . on the whole our divines have written, because they were obliged to write, and so far as they were obliged. They have written answers to particular assailants, have grown out of pamphlets into folios, and, like great musicians, have worked out profound movements from subjects which the chance of the moment offered. Thus the works of Jewell, Bramhall, Horsley, and Waterland, are in great measure the gradual increase of controversy with a disputant, developing itself in fresh replies, handling and elaborating the same matter again and again.[12]

In November 1834, Hampden sent Newman his recent pamphlet advocating the admission of religious dissenters into the university.[13] Why should they, he asked, be disbarred because they hold different theological opinions? After all, doctrines are only the "conclusions of human reasoning," no matter how "logically sound" and "correctly deduced" they are. Strictly speaking, they are not "religious truths." Revealed truth bears no resemblance to that "dogmatical and sententious wisdom" created by "theological controversy."[14] Conclusions from scripture cannot be treated with the same reverence as those "truths" which scripture itself "simply declares."[15] Speculations are not "parts of revelation" and must not be mistaken as "genuine mintage."[16] The Church of England is "neither dogmatic in its spirit . . . nor intolerant and sectarian in its zeal." Its aim is to unite "as many hearts and voices as possible in one common confession, without exacting a rigid and impossible uniformity of opinion from individual members."[17] Newman promptly informed Hampden that the pamphlet made "shipwreck" of Christianity and would disrupt the traditional peace and harmony of Oxford. Thirty years later, he singled it out as the first salvo fired by Anglican liberalism on the "old orthodoxy of Oxford and England."[18]

At the time, Newman was assembling a second volume of sermons for publication. Within a fortnight of receiving the pamphlet, he wrote five additional sermons, apparently to counter some of Hampden's statements, and included them in the forthcoming volume. They are dated 11 December 1834. Although they do not mention Hampden by name, there is no doubt what was in Newman's mind. What is unique about these sermons is that Newman never preached them.

In "Mysteries in Religion," "The Indwelling Spirit," "The Gospel, a Trust Committed to Us," "Tolerance of Religious Error," and "Christian Zeal" he insists that mystery touches every moment of our lives.[19] Instead of treating the articles of the creed as of doubtful relevance because they are mysterious and beyond human understanding, we should receive them with wonder, awe, and gratitude. We do not have to understand them to believe them. We must silently worship, jealously protect and faithfully preserve them. Since it is the work of the Holy Spirit, we cannot afford to treat God's revealed word lightly. In tampering with it, we are tampering with the work of the Holy Spirit.

Our faith is a reservoir of theological propositions that is one and the same in every age. We do not have to search because the Holy Spirit gives them to us in baptism. Every article of the creed can be ascertained from scripture and each is a sacred trust committed to our keeping. Therefore, we must never gloss over them carelessly, systematize them simplistically, or dismiss them as pious nonsense. We have a duty to preserve the creed for posterity. The growing trend was to say that the creed and its articles of faith are unenlightened opinions, that they damage real religion, that belief in them is superstitious, and that they interfere with individual Christian freedom.

The Church has always taught that scripture contains a definite number of revealed propositions. These include, though not always explicitly, the Trinity and the Incarnation; Christ's mediatorship and atonement on

Calvary; his death, burial, resurrection, and ascension; the forgiveness of sin; baptism; the laying on of hands; and the resurrection of the dead and general judgment. Instead of treating them as sacred mysteries, some teachers think that their duty is to strip them of their mysteriousness and separate the practical from the impractical, the relevant from the irrelevant.

Hampden, on the other hand, believed that scripture alone is the "sole oracle" of revealed truth, not tradition, not the Church.[20] Revelation consists of facts that must be "equally received and followed as true." Religious doctrines are of human origin and, therefore, limited and flawed. They are open to rational scrutiny and can be "variously held *without danger to salvation.*"[21] This includes the Thirty-nine Articles, the Nicene Creed, and the Athanasian Creed.[22] Doctrines are the "remnants" of a metaphysically and logically flawed theology.[23] Tradition is important, but it carries no "*divine* authority." It is a "guide," not an "oracle."[24] While any doctrine corroborated by tradition "demands our most serious attention" and while we should respect the Fathers of the Church, we are not obliged to "accept their estimate of its value." Nevertheless, certain "*revealed facts,*" about which there is "no rational doubt," do exist—namely: that human nature is basically corrupt; that Christ came to redeem us and bring "Life and Immortality"; that he was crucified for our sins and rose for our justification; and that the Holy Spirit lives in the heart of every sincere Christian. "There is enough in them to warm and comfort the heart, though we had assurance of nothing more."[25]

The main difficulty with the Trinity comes about because of the technical language invented to talk about it. The real truth "emerges from these mists of human speculation, like the bold, naked land, on which an atmosphere of fog has for a while rested, and then been dispersed." Certainly, there is "a real mystery" about the Christian God, but there is also an unnecessary one "attached to the subject, which is not a mystery of God." It is one superimposed by scholastic theology. Reality should not be confused with theory.[26] Apart from the events themselves, scripture makes no dogmatic statements regarding the Incarnation, atonement, or justification. Original sin is a theory to explain human corruption while the teaching of the soul's separate existence is a relic of scholasticism. The idea of a sacramental system is "utterly repugnant to the spirit of Christianity," while the idea of sacramental "influence" goes back to the early Church and the "general belief" in magic.[27] Only the Protestant reformers had "courage to break that charm which the mystical number of the Sacraments carried with it." In their own limited way, dogmatic formulas perform a utilitarian function. Even with its acknowledged imperfections, a "system of technical theology" acts as a buffer against the "exorbitance of theoretic enthusiasm" and a bulwark against those who would eradicate it altogether. Such a system establishes "their importance and proper truth, as distinct from the honour and variety of the simple Divine Word."[28]

Many were outraged by Hampden's nomination to the Regius Professorship of Divinity. He would be entrusted with the education of a generation of Anglican clergy. Because "continued silence" could be interpreted as the seal of approval, Newman published *Elucidations on Dr Hampden's Theological Statements* to expose what he thought to be the implications of Hampden's principles as expressed in his 1832 Bampton lectures and his 1834 pamphlet on dissenters. His strategy was simplicity itself, although it has been the subject of fierce criticism ever since.[29] From these two sources, he selected statements representative of Hampden's theological opinions, adding brief comments but not, however, going as far as to accuse him of heresy.

Privately, he did. In fact, Hampden was worse than one. "There is no doctrine, however sacred, which he does not scoff at." As for his moral philosophy, "he adopts the lowest and most grovelling utilitarianism." And as for Hampden himself, "this man, *judging by his writings*, is the most lucre loving, earthly minded, unlovely person one ever set eyes on." By comparison, "Arnold is amiable and winning."[30]

One prominent Tractarian, however, did accuse Hampden of "heresy" in an open letter.[31] Baden Powell rallied to Hampden's defence and launched an attack on Tractarians generally, describing some of their statements as "more like the reveries of visionaries and the hallucinations of fanatics than the sober deliberations of academical divines."[32] Their tactics reminded him of the Inquisition. As he saw it, the nation was faced with several principles of "momentous practical importance." Namely, whether the theology student should be "*encouraged to think for himself*"; "whether belief shall rest on *conviction*"; whether theology should be taught on the "basis of rational enquiry"; and "whether CHRISTIANITY shall stand on the foundation of TRUTH."[33]

Tractarians, he continued, carry on as if they have a monopoly on truth and as if they represent the Church. They cannot see that they are only one party among many in a much wider Church. The Church of England is "moderation and liberality." It is big enough to accommodate not only those "votaries of infallibility," but all "those of various shades of more rational opinions." The Church and the universities will be best served if more men of Hampden's calibre are appointed to "high and responsible positions" in these establishments. "The appointment to these stations of men possessing alike the essential qualification of entertaining such views, joined with the ability to support, and the moral courage to maintain them, affords the only hope of effecting any improvement."[34]

Like Hampden, Baden Powell believed that the Gospels are the one, authentic, authoritative depository of God's word. There is no other "collateral channel" for interpreting "*their contents*."[35] The Gospels contain no "precise" creeds, only "comprehensive truths," and no "systematic laws," only "practical principles." No external authority can replace the primacy of private judgment. Only to the extent that anything is "*clearly revealed*," does religion exist. Any suspicion that something may be hidden is the "spirit of mysticism." To those who believe that Christianity is "fully and finally" revealed in the Gospels, the "dubious twilight of mystical devotion, and the vague apprehension of the unrevealed mysteries" are surely at odds with the "very nature of Christianity."[36] Toleration of religious mystery is "destructive of all sound and rational belief" and a convenient "cloak to cover total unbelief and confirmed irreligion."[37] To a "simple believer in the written word of the New Testament, the system of tradition" erases "all distinctive characteristics" of a definite deposit and "*destroys* the whole evidence of the Gospel."[38] Creeds and "formularies" have a legitimate niche in the Church provided we remember that they are "human synopses and fallible expositions, and subject always . . . to the written word *alone*, for their interpretation and warrant." Their "chief recommendation" is not their "*antiquity*" but their "*utility*."[39] Otherwise, people who "follow antiquity as the surest guide to revelation" will start to see "Christianity anywhere *except* in the New Testament."[40]

Whately and Newman had been drifting apart, socially and theologically. For some time, Newman had been uneasy about the "dangerous" drift of his old mentor's principles.[41] He warned Whately that they could seriously erode the "very fundamentals" of every religious argument and damage "almost every doctrine and every maxim by which our faith or our conduct is to be guided."[42]

In *Omission of Creeds*, Whately suggests that the Apostles' Creed is not a summary of fundamentals of the Christian faith but a confession of faith, "intended to ascertain the professed orthodoxy of those who adopt it." Because of its "acknowledged antiquity" and its apostolical tradition, many people venerate it to the point of superstition by reciting it as a prayer. Anyone who does is obviously ignorant of "its general drift." The problem of prayer is its habit of "degenerating into a superstitious formalism," particularly "with a Liturgy transmitted to us from the time of the Apostles, as a part of Scripture."[43] The same goes for catechisms. No prescribed code of doctrines or way of teaching Christianity can be universally and permanently effective. That is why each local Church is left to "steer its own course by the Chart and Compass which his holy Word supplies, regulating for itself the Sails and Rudder, according to the winds and currents it may meet with."[44]

Christ entrusted the "office of *teaching*" to the whole Church and the office of "*proving*" its doctrines to scripture. To the local Church, however, he left the "*application*" of those principles in their articles of faith, liturgy and Church law.[45] As for that vast collection of writings by "*uninspired* writers" throughout the ages, there should be no scruple about changing them when and where necessary. Since they are uninspired, they provide a dramatic contrast between the "compositions of fallible" people and the "admirable provisions" of divine wisdom. God has revealed the "knowledge of what we could not have discovered for ourselves," but "has left us to ourselves precisely in those points in which it is best for us that we should be so left."[46] While it is conceivable for a local Church or individual to be "*free* from error," no Church or individual can be completely "*secure* from error," either now or in the future. While we are not bound to doubt the doctrines we now hold, we must be constantly scrutinizing scripture for error. Neither Church nor individual is infallible and it is dangerous "arrogance" to think so.[47] Christians must "*examine* and re-examine" the reasons for holding any doctrines with the same intensity as if they suspected them of being wrong. "The skilful and cautious navigator keeps his reckoning with care, but never so far trusts to that as not *to keep a look-out* . . . and to take *an observation* when opportunity offers." While this regular cycle of critical re-examination is going on, we have to carry on and act according to our religious convictions as if "certain of their being correct."[48] The best insurance against error is not blind faith but a well developed habit of "self-distrust, and perpetual care, and diligent watchfulness, and openness to conviction."[49]

The sign of authentic revelation is its "exclusively *practical*" nature. Otherwise, it is a "*pretended*" revelation, such as the "fables of the Jewish Talmud" and that "multitude of idle legends" scattered throughout the Roman Church, "which have no more reference to practice" than heathen mythology.[50] The bulk has no "conceivable" relevance to life except to titillate the "roving imagination, and gratify the presumptuous curiosity of the credulous." Any religion that smacks of a curious and arcane nature and preaches religious mystery is either the "obvious" ploy of a fraud, the ravings of a visionary, or the "dupe" of its "own distempered fancy."[51]

To preserve the "practical tendency" of revelation and to ensure that nothing is included "to pamper vain curiosity," Whately sets out a few simple guidelines. First, no single historical event in scripture can "strictly or properly" be considered a "point of miraculous revelation." Even "*taken collectively*," they are no more than "highly instructive," and fall far short of that standard of practicality "which we are authorized to expect." The characteristic of a genuine revelation is its stark brevity, which leaves the inquirer's curiosity unsatisfied. Such is the Mosaic account of creation. All that is revealed for practical purposes is that there is one God.[52] Second, although we may not "understand the *ultimate* purpose of any part of our revelation, still, if we perceive an *immediate* purpose that is practical," we must not confuse it with that of a "supposed revelation which has no perceptible purpose at all." That is, if it is clear that "something is to be done in consequence of what is revealed, even though we may not understand why that particular duty *should* be enjoined, still the revelation is evidently practical."[53] Third, some revelation may have had a practical application for a particular period or person, but that does not mean it is universally pertinent. Finally, it behoves each Christian to become morally better persons. By adopting the "most *practical* interpretation of each doctrine," we can be sure that it is, in all probability, the right one. Beyond that, "purely speculative" doctrines are irrelevant.[54]

Owing to his influence on Whately and Hampden, Joseph Blanco White is "sometimes considered a founder of modern latitudinarianism in the Church of England."[55] Newman once told Gladstone that White was a "fastidiously honourable man, in word and deed," but "never a patient, careful thinker." He had "very little of practical judgment" and sometimes acted on the spur of the moment. Like most liberals, he "loved and sought truth" in the same way "as mathematicians love and seek mathematical truth . . . *without fearing error*."[56] Hence, "he was not afraid of theological mistakes." He

> . . . had no *proposition* before his mind—but I thought he *acted out* a position, the same arguments which brought him down one step forcing him down the next. It was "If I give up a, I must give up b; but if I give up b, I must give up c, and so on."[57]

He abandoned Roman Catholicism, became an Anglican, adopted rationalism, embraced Unitarianism, and died a pantheist,

> . . . denying that there is an ultra-mundane God, apparently denying a particular Providence, doubting, to say the least, the personal immortality of the soul, meditating from Marcus Antoninus, and considering that

St Paul's epistles are taken from the Stoic philosophy. As to Christianity he seems thoroughly to agree with Strauss, and rejects the gospels as historical documents.[58]

In 1835 White published *Heresy and Orthodoxy*, declaring his Unitarianism and attacking Protestantism. He renounced the Thirty-nine Articles and the Trinity, dismissed patristic theology as "groundless speculations."[59] As for Protestantism's fundamental rule of scripture and private judgment, there is "no revealed *rule* . . . to ascertain, with moral certainty, which doctrines are right and which are wrong." In fact, the very "absence of a *rule*" is divine proof that the gospel alone is the appointed road to happiness and salvation. Furthermore,

> . . . SALVATION cannot depend on ORTHODOXY. The gospel cannot consist in abstract doctrines, about which men of equal abilities, virtue, and sincerity, are, and have always been, divided. Once establish this principle, and the objection which, on the supposition of Orthodoxy, irresistibly opposes revelation, is instantly rendered powerless.[60]

There are no universal guidelines to distinguish "*essential* and *non-essential*" doctrines.[61] Christ did not intend "doctrinal unity."[62] He invites us "to cast off the yoke of statutes and ordinances of all kinds relating to religion."[63] Christianity is a call to freedom, not bondage.

The Holy Spirit is the promised guide to the mind of every sincere Christian. Whatever theories of revelation and inspiration are propounded, we are assured that reason must be convinced of their truth. Otherwise, madness and reason become indistinguishable: "Every thing *not reasonable*, either in itself, or by virtue of the *ground* upon which we accept it, is *absurd*. REVELATION can have no authority for a rational being, till REASON has recognised it as such."[64]

God intended the Gospels to "perpetuate some historical facts concerning Christ and his apostles" and to provide guidelines for the Christian life. What these are, is providentially entrusted to the private judgment of each individual. God never promised an orthodox infallible authority, only "individual guidance."[65] By its very definition, revelation means the "*disclosure*" of something both real and rational. It does not include "downright contradictions" or "*mysterious words*, which, like the ABRACADABRA of the Gnostics, is to save us from evil by the sound and shape of its letters. There is a vast difference "between mysteries *to be explained* and mysteries *to be proved*":

> Reason submits to the former, because the existence of the mysterious fact is unquestionable; but when called upon to submit to the latter,

because forsooth they also are *mysteries*, it turns away in disgust. The mysteries to which the reason of the Unitarian objects are not mysteries *proved*, are not even mysteries positively stated in divinely authorized language, but mysteries *conjectured* to lie concealed in that language: they are not unfrequently *verbal contradictions*, which no rational language can be supposed to contain.[66]

Scholasticism has had a damaging impact on the Gospels. Its original message has become "thickly incrusted with the most vague, incorrect, and vulgar notions." Christians have always two options. Either they can blindly accept a "superstitious and indiscriminate" belief system or they can reject "the subject as totally unworthy of attention."[67] Not only is Christ a "SAVIOUR from SIN," he is also a saviour from "SUPERSTITION." That includes "all religions which make ceremonies and a priesthood essential to spiritual safety."[68]

> TRUTH . . . means *reality*, in contradistinction to *emblems*; the worship of the heart, in opposition to the worship of ceremonies; the direct worship of the soul, not that which requires the interposition of a priesthood . . . the only acceptable worship must be that which is truly *spiritual*. Figures and ceremonies must cease; for they are shadows, and he [God] loves realities. The only sacrifice he demands is that of the individual will to his supreme will. This is the *reasonable service* of faith, peculiar to Christianity.[69]

No "candid and reasonable" person will deny that articles of faith are the "work of *reason*," and not the "result of *inspiration*." Protestants have to admit that the explanation of scripture as set out in "their respective creeds, is a work of reason, or they must embrace the Popish principle of infallibility."[70] Any middle ground is "untenable and self-contradictory."[71] White rejected the position of Anglicanism as "diluted Popery." His rejection, Newman suspected, arose out of "hatred" and "personal resentment" against the Church of Rome:

> It was a deep, awful, personal feeling . . . the Church of Rome had, he considered, been the bane of his life—she was his enemy[,] he never forgave her. Every thing which reminded him of her was involved in the antipathy. People used to say when he became a Unitarian, "O he will go round to his old Church at last"—I always said he never would. It was not a matter of argument, system, religion. Rome never could be his friend—he had an argument against her within him closer than any conceivable persuasive.[72]

In addition to liberal Anglicans, Newman thought ultra-Protestants could also introduce rational principles into revealed religion. Although not having the same spirit as a Hampden or a Whately, he was of the opinion that they had a habit of focussing on feelings, without paying attention to "anything external," such as "creed, actions, or ritual." This was a "specious form of trusting man rather than God" and, by its nature, rationalistic.[73] Among ultra-Protestantism's "most influential" and "most original" representatives, Newman singled out Thomas Erskine, a moderate Scottish churchman with an Evangelical cast of mind, and Jacob Abbott, an American Congregationalist minister, neither of whom would ever have considered themselves liberal. For Newman, they were advocating a disguised form of rationalism which could lead to scepticism just as surely as Anglican liberalism did. Such was the "twofold genius" of rationalism.[74]

Their notion was that the atonement was the "corner-stone of Christianity" to which every other doctrine was automatically subservient.[75] If this were so, the Incarnation was "necessary and important" only to the extent that it lent sacredness to the atonement. Likewise, the Trinity was important only to the extent that it revealed the Holy Spirit, "by whose aid and influence the Gospel message" was transmitted:

It follows that faith is nearly the whole of religious service, for through it the message or Manifestation is received; on the other hand, the scientific language of Catholicism, concerning the Trinity and the Incarnation, is disparaged, as having no tendency to enforce the effect upon our minds of the doctrine of the Atonement, while the Sacraments are limited to the office of representing, and promising, and impressing on us the promise of divine influences, in no measure of conveying them. Thus the Dispensation, in its length, depth, and height, is practically identified with its Revelation, or rather its necessarily superficial Manifestation. Not that the reality of the Atonement, in itself, is formally denied, but it is cast in the background, except so far as it can be discovered to be influential, viz., to show God's hatred of sin, the love of Christ, and the like; and there is an evident tendency to consider it as a *mere* Manifestation of the love of Christ, to the denial of all real virtue in it as an expiation for sin; as if His death took place merely to show His love for us as a sign of God's infinite mercy, to calm and assure us, without any real connexion existing between it and God's forgiveness of our sins. And the Dispensation thus being hewn and chiselled into an intelligible human system, is represented, when thus mutilated, as affording a remarkable evidence of the truth of the Bible, an evidence level to the reason, and superseding the testimony of the Apostles.[76]

As for the atonement's alleged superiority over other doctrines, Newman thought that each revealed truth has its assigned position in the system and no truth can be moved "one inch" or made subservient to another. "There is a difference between being prominent and being paramount."[77] While Erskine preferred to talk about the atonement as a "great and glorious" manifestation to our reason of God's justice, Newman preferred to talk about it as an "ever mysterious" event, addressed to our faith but not to our reason. "If you ask me," wrote Newman,

> I do not believe we are informed that Christ's death is a satisfaction to God's *justice*—This is going beyond Scripture, to show *how* it is a satisfaction. It is a satisfaction in that it propitiates His wrath—*how* His wrath is put away is not revealed—to say it is by His justice being satisfied, I suspect, is a Calvinistic gloss. If Scripture says it, I receive it as a mystery (which Mr Erskine *would not* do) a mystery as great in its way as the Trinity—for how God's *justice* . . . could be satisfied by one suffering for another, is past my conception.[78]

Newman took issue with Erskine's suggestion that the "reasonableness of a religion" consisted in there being a direct, natural, and intelligible link between belief in a doctrine and the formation of a person's moral character in the likeness of God. According to him, if no such link existed, then there was a "very strong probability" militating against the "truth of that religion."[79] The object of Christian revelation is to "bring the character of man into harmony with that of God."[80] According to Newman, however, God may well have intended "us to partake in His moral likeness," but to suggest that it was "the *leading idea*," was "unwarranted," "presumptuous," and smacked of rationalism.[81] Such assumptions can only "disparage, if not supersede," the great mysteries of revelation.[82] According to Erskine, the Trinity was practical insofar as it manifested God's "moral character." And insofar as it was a part of a creed, it was abstract, unreasonable, unimportant, and not worthy of belief. Erskine

> . . . has cut out the *Doctrine* by its roots, and has preserved only that superficial part of it which he denominates a "*Manifestation*,"—only so much as bears visibly upon another part of the system, our moral character,—so much as is perceptibly connected with it,—so much as may be comprehended.[83]

In expressing the mystery of the Incarnation, Newman thought that "we should rather say that God is man than that man is God." The first proposition tends to restrict Christ's personality to his divine nature while making his humanity an "adjunct." The second proposition goes in exactly the opposite direction. By focussing too much on it, Erskine and Abbott gave the impression that Christ is "primarily and personally" a man, "with some vast and unknown dignity superadded, and that acquired of course after His coming into existence as man."[84] Jacob Abbott seemed to come "within a hair's breadth of Socinianism" by treating Christ as nothing more than an extraordinary human being who was uniquely "aided and blessed by God." He seemed to think that Christ exhibited divine attributes in the same way as the "solar system manifests His power," and the animal kingdom, God's wisdom. Not only did it look like a "poorly concealed Socinianism," it had distinct pantheistic overtones.[85] He seemed to treat "the Almighty, not as the Great God, but as some vast physical and psychological phenomenon," with no other existence independent of creation. Thus, the Incarnation was nothing but a "moral" manifestation of God in the person of Jesus Christ. As far as Newman was concerned, Abbott made no distinction between "the manifestation of God in Christ, and the manifestation of Him in a plant or flower."[86] As for the atonement, its value seemed to rest on the "moral effect" of Christ's death, rather than on expiation and reconciliation. Such theologizing "violently robs the Christian Creed of all it contains, except those outward historical facts through which its divine truths were fulfilled and revealed" to us.[87]

In spite of his opposition to liberal Anglicanism and ultra-Protestantism, Newman favoured reason in theological investigations, provided it respected boundaries. It is not rationalism, for example, to ascertain what matters are "attainable by reason, and what are not." And where there has been no express revelation, it is not rationalism to investigate the truths of natural religion, or to devise valid proofs to test their authenticity. Likewise, if insufficient proof is available, then it is not rationalism to reject that revelation. Once recognized as a genuine revelation, it is not rationalism to "investigate the meaning of its declarations, and to interpret its language." And it is not rationalism to bring revealed truths "into dependence on each other, to trace their mutual relations, and to pursue them to their legitimate issues."[88]

It is rationalism, however, to accept revelation and proceed to explain it away, to speak of it as the word of God and treat it as the word of a human being. It is also rationalism to refuse revelation the right to speak for itself and "to claim to be told the *why* and the *how* of God's dealings with us" and then proceed to interpret it privately. It is also rationalism to balk at what God had revealed because of its incompleteness or obscurity or to insist that the "contents" of revelation are also "its proof." And it is rationalism "to frame some gratuitous hypothesis about them, and then to garble, gloss, and to colour them, to trim, clip, pare away, and twist them, in order to bring them into conformity with the idea to which we have subjected them."[89]

Notes

1. R. Brent, *Liberal Anglican Politics: Whiggery, Religion, and Reform*, pp. 145-7. For a stimulating account of the liberal Anglican idea of history, see D. Forbes, *The Liberal Idea of History* (Cambridge, 1952).

2. J. H. Overton, *The English Church in the Nineteenth Century*, pp. 110-1.

3. *Ibid.* "Noetic" comes from Aristotle's *Nicomachean Ethics* (Book VI). A Noetic was someone who exercised his intellectual faculties to the highest possible degree in contrast to someone who let them lie dormant. Politically, Noetics were "not uniformly Whiggish in a partisan sense." Whately, for example, always claimed exemption from "Whiggery and Toryism & such like infirmities" (Brent, *op.cit.*, pp. 146-7).

4. Brent, *op. cit.*, p. 150.

5. R. D. Hampden, *The Scholastic Philosophy Considered in its Relation to Christian Theology* (Oxford, 1833), p. 13.

6. *Apo.*, pp. 288-90.

7. Edward Burton (1794-1836).

8. *L.D.* IV, 320.

9. *L.D.* V, 120; 122; 126.

10. *Ibid.*, pp. 120-1.

11. *Ibid.*, pp. 50-1.

12. *Ess.* I, 179-80.

13.Hampden, *Observations on Religious Dissent with Particular Reference to the Use of Religious Tests in the University* (second edition, Oxford, 1834).

14. *Ibid.*, pp. 7-8.

15. *Ibid.*, p. 11.

16. *Ibid.*, pp. 13-4.

17. *Ibid.*, pp. 22-3.

18. *Apo.*, pp. 57-8.

19. *P.S.* II, 206-16; 217-31; 255-73; 274-90; 379-92.

20. Hampden, *A Lecture on Tradition* (London, 1839), pp. 18; 21-2.

21. Hampden, *Scholastic Philosophy Considered*, pp. 373-4; 352-3.

22. *Ibid.*, p. 378.

23. *Ibid.*, pp. 155; 352; 380; 384.

24. Hampden, *A Lecture on Tradition* (Oxford, 1833), pp. 8; 10; 38.

25. Hampden, *Scholastic Philosophy Considered*, pp. 390-1.

26. *Ibid.*, pp. 145-6; 150.

27. *Ibid.*, pp. 221-2; 310-1; 315; 341-2. Thomas Arnold (1795-1842) was also a liberal Anglican. He maintained that the idea of a "human priesthood" was invented amidst the turmoils of the second century. The Church

> . . . pretended that the clergy were not simply rulers and teachers, . . . but that they were essentially mediators between God and the church, . . . so the clergy began to draw to themselves the attributes of the church, and to call the church by a different name, such as the faithful, or the laity; so that to speak of the church mediating for the people did not sound so shocking, and the doctrine so disguised found ready acceptance. Thus the evil work was consummated; the great majority of the members of the church were virtually disfranchised; the minority retained the name, but the character of the institution was utterly corrupted (*Christian Life, its Course, its Hindrances, and its Helps*, fourth edition, London, 1845, pp. li-lii).

28. *Ibid.*, pp. 342; 380; 383; 375-6.

29. *V.M.* II, 189; *Apo.*, pp. 57-8.

30. *L.D.* V, p. 251. One of the characters in Newman's 1848 novel, *Loss and Gain*, was a certain Doctor Brownside who was the new dean of Nottingham, a former Huntingdonian Professor of Divinity and one of the "acutest" and "soundest" academics of the day. The description of Brownside reads like a caricature of Hampden:

> Revelation to him, instead of being the abyss of God's counsels, with its dim outlines and broad shadows, was a flat sunny plain, laid out with straight macadamised roads. Not . . . that he denied the Divine incomprehensibility itself, with certain heretics of old; but he maintained that in Revelation all that was mysterious had been left out, and nothing given us but what was practical, and directly concerned us. It was, moreover, to him a marvel, that everyone did not agree with him in taking this simple, natural view, which he thought almost self-evident; and he attributed the phenomenon, which was by no means uncommon, to some want of clearness of head, or twist of mind (*L.G.* pp. 67-8).

31. B. Powell, *Remarks on a Letter from the Rev. H. A. Woodgate to Viscount Melbourne, Relative to the Appointment of Dr. Hampden* (Oxford,1837), pp. 6-7. The Tractarian was Henry Arthur Woodgate (1801-74), one of Newman's closest friends at the time and fellow of St John's College. His open letter was published on 31 March 1836. At the time, Baden Powell (1796-1860) was Savilian Professor of Geometry at Oxford.

32. Powell, *Remarks on a Letter*, pp. 4; 6-7; 10.

33. *Ibid.*, p. 20.

34. *Ibid.*, pp. 21-2.

35. Powell, *Tradition Unveiled: or, An Exposition of the Pretensions and Tendency of Authoritative Teaching in the Church* (London, 1839), pp. 70-1.

36. *Ibid.*, pp. 74-6.

37. *Ibid.*, pp. 62; 64.

38. *Ibid.*, pp. 68-9.

39. *Ibid.*, p. 72.

40. *Ibid.*, pp. 48-9.

41. Very soon, he was warning people about the dangerous principles of Whately's *Omission of Creeds*. See BOA B. 3. 4., Sermon 347; preached at the Ambassador's Chapel, Naples, on 14 April 1833, and on three subsequent occasions at Oxford and Littlemore.

42. *Apo.*, p. 382. By 1833, relations were so strained that Newman admitted that "I really doubt whether I ought to sit down to table with him, if I were in his neighbourhood (*L.D.* IV, 27).

43. Whately, *An Essay on the Omission of Creeds, Liturgies and Codes of Ecclesiastical Canons in the New Testament* (London, 1831), pp. 27-9. See *G.A.*, pp. 132-4.

44. *Ibid.*, pp. 29-30.

45. *Ibid.*, p. 37.

46. *Ibid.*, pp. 37-8.

47. *Ibid.*, pp. 47-8.

48. *Ibid.*, p. 49.

49. *Ibid.*, p. 51.

50. Whately, *Essays on Some of the Peculiarities of the Christian Religion* (Oxford, 1825), p. 184.

51. *Ibid.*, pp. 192-3.

52. *Ibid.*, pp. 197-9.

53. *Ibid.*, pp. 201-2.

54. *Ibid.*, pp. 215; 218-9. Although Thomas Arnold was a liberal Anglican, Newman admired his great work at Rugby and considered him "widely different from Whately, Hawkins, and

many other persons with whom he is associated, as more real and earnest than his friends, as having done a work, when they are merely talkers" (BOA Letter to John Keble from Littlemore, 12 Sept. 1842). See *L.D.* XXV, 325.

55. M. Svaglic (ed.), *Apologia pro Vita Sua*, p. 486.

56. BOA Letter to W. E. Gladstone, 12 June 1845.

57. BOA Letter to W. E. Gladstone, 17 June, 1845.

58. BOA Letter to W. E. Gladstone, 27 April 1845.

59. B. White, *Observations on Heresy and Orthodoxy* (London,1835), p. v.

60. *Ibid.*, pp. 10-1.

61. *Ibid.*, p. vii.

62. *Ibid.*, p. 13.

63. *Ibid.*, p. 52.

64. *Ibid.*, pp. 58-9.

65. *Ibid.*, p. 71.

66. *Ibid.*, pp. 97-8.

67. *Ibid.*, pp. 21-2.

68. *Ibid.*, p. 41.

69. *Ibid.*, p. 45. "Faith without reason," wrote Thomas Arnold, "is not properly faith, but mere power worship; and power worship may be devil worship" (L. Trilling, *Matthew Arnold*, p. 57).

70. *Ibid.*, p. 86.

71. [R. H. Froude], "Mr Blanco White, Heresy and Orthodoxy," *British Critic*, Vol. XIX, January 1836, p. 219.

72. BOA Letter to W. E. Gladstone, 12 June 1845. See Ward I, 80. Newman's attitude to White was always one of kindness and compassion: "Yet, I do not understand why, though it is thirteen years since I saw him, and I only had one letter from him since, his image haunts me more than the dearest friends whom I have lost, and I can fancy him before me, and have a vivid impression of his voice, countenance and manner" (*Ibid.*).

73. *Ess.* I, 95-6.

74. R. H. Froude, *Remains*, Vol. I, Part the Second, p. 2. In 1834, Newman wrote a paper for J. F. Christie (1808-60) analyzing the ideas of the Scottish churchman, Thomas Chalmers (1780-1847). In it, he makes the point that current Evangelicalism and liberalism shared much in common, including the tendency to make revealed truths reasonable and practical (BOA A. 9. 1, "Critical Remarks upon Dr Chalmer's [sic] Theology").

75. T. Erskine, *Remarks on the Internal Evidences*, p. 97.

76. *Ess.* I, 47-8. By "*manifestation*," Newman understood Erskine to mean the act of "making the *reason* of it *intelligible*" (*Ess.* I, 66n).

77. *Ibid.*, p. 65.

78. *L.D.* V, 336-7.

79. Erskine, *Remarks on the Internal Evidences*, p. 59.

80. *Ibid.*, p. 49.

81. *Ess.* I, 53.

82. *Ibid.*, p. 54.

83. *Ibid.*, p. 57. See C. Gunton, "Newman's Dialectic: Dogma and Reason in the Seventy-Third Tracts for the Times," pp. 309-22, in *Newman after a Hundred Years*, I. Ker and A. G. Hill (eds.) (Oxford, 1990).

84. *Ibid.*, p. 74.

85. *Ibid.*, pp. 72ff.

86. *Ibid.*, pp. 78ff.

87. *Ibid.*, pp. 84ff.
88. *Ibid.*, p. 32.
89. *Ibid.* One of Newman's earliest biographers was Wilfrid Ward (1856-1916). Ward once suggested that, like most great writers, Newman developed his classical style by an intensity of thought that energized his theological world view. His "brooding imagination" stemmed from a "deep and hard-won conviction" and not from some cleverness of articulation. His style conveyed personal "suffering and labour" and a "sense of triumph at conviction laboriously won." The experience possessed him totally and broadened his theological horizons considerably. His voice was like the "deep note" of some "great bell" sounding "the solemn lesson of his own life" (*Last Lectures*, London, 1918, p. 50).

CHAPTER 5

God's Message to the Heathen: Anglican Years

The development of Newman's understanding of universal revelation happened in three stages. In the first he explains the principle, without having to defend it, in sermons, in a personal memorandum and in *Arians of the Fourth Century*. In the second, during which the Oxford Movement was at its height, he defends the idea against liberalism's neglect of a universal revelation; as he explores its possibilities in tracts, lectures, and articles, the tone of his writing becomes more confident, the language sharper, and the insights more incisive. Finally, in the writing of *Essay on Development*, he uses the idea to illustrate the Church's gift to adapt rites and customs from other religions into its liturgy and teaching.

"Dispensation of paganism" was one of several terms he initially used to refer to universal revelation but did not persevere with. The first time was in the second University Sermon, where he argues that no religious system had ever been established by "unaided" reason.[1] Although only a "portion of the world" had been gifted with an "authenticated revelation," no race of people has ever been denied one from God.[2] Classical literature attests to the actual religious state of many pagans and to a "practical" creed of natural religion of which personal conscience is the "essential principle and sanction of Religion in the mind"[3]:

> Conscience implies a relation between the soul and a something exterior, and that, moreover, superior to itself; a relation to an excellence which it does not possess, and to a tribunal over which it has no power. And since the more closely this inward monitor is respected and followed, the clearer, the more exalted, and the more varied its dictates become, and the standard of excellence is ever outstripping, while it guides, our obedience, a moral conviction is thus at length obtained of the unapproachable nature as well as the supreme authority of That, whatever it is, which is the object of the mind's contemplation. Here, then, at once, we have the elements of a religious system; for what is Religion, but the system of relations existing between us and a Supreme Power, claiming our habitual obedience.[4]

Furthermore, conscience forcibly offers each person the prospect of eternal life and a final judgment of present behaviour. This "inward law" supplies "no proof of its truth" but commands attention and demands complete obedience. It is one of the principal ways by which God reveals the truths of natural religion. A well-informed conscience

> . . . habitually and honestly conforming itself to its own full sense of duty, will at length enjoin or forbid with an authority second only to an inspired oracle. Moreover, in a heathen country, it will be able to discriminate with precision between the right and wrong in traditionary superstitions, and will thus elicit confirmation of its faith even out of corruptions of the truth. And further, it will of course realize in its degree those peculiar rewards of virtue which appetite cannot comprehend; and will detect in this world's events . . . a general connexion existing between right moral conduct and happiness, in corroboration of those convictions which the experience of its own private history has created.[5]

Such a large, practical creed is attainable by any vigorous conscientious mind under the divine aegis of a "Dispensation of Paganism." It is even conceivable that there is no "essential character of Scripture doctrine which is without its place in this moral revelation." By themselves, they are a limited means to a limited end. Although natural religion teaches something about God's "infinite power and majesty," "wisdom and goodness," "moral governance," and "unity," it offers very little information about God's "*Personality*." Although infinitely great, this God remains a metaphysical abstraction and less than a God of love. By telling us simple, concrete stories about the life, death, and resurrection of Jesus Christ, the Gospels supply the missing information and so satisfy the tensions and yearnings of the human heart:

> The life of Christ brings together and concentrates truths concerning the chief good and the laws of our being, which wander idle and forlorn over the surface of the moral world, and often appear to diverge from each other. It collects the scattered rays of light, which, in the first days of creation, were poured over the whole face of nature, into certain intelligible centres, in the firmament of the heaven, to rule over the day and over the night, and to divide the light from the darkness. Our Saviour has in Scripture all those abstract titles of moral excellence bestowed upon Him which philosophers have invented. He is the Word, the Light, the Life, the Truth, Wisdom, the Divine Glory St. John announces in the text, "The Life was manifested, and we *have seen* It."[6]

In 1830 Newman wrote a long letter to his brother Charles on revelation. As a postscript, he had added a memorandum, which he decided not to send, "for it would not profit him now," but "may at some future day." He begins:

I believe in an *universal* revelation—the doctrines of which are preserved by tradition in the world at large, in Scripture in the Christian Church. The only difference in this respect between us and the heathen nations, is, that *we* have a written, *they* an unwritten memorial of it. Not that the world in a religious point of view is simply divisible into two classes. Revelation is a gift, like all gifts, diffused with indefinite inequality all over the earth. In the Apostolical Church itself it varies indefinitely in its degree—the Romanists have far less of a revelation than we have. In like manner Islamism in its different forms, and Polytheism besides in its numberless varieties, contain revelations from God.—I do not say they *are* revelations, but they *embody* revealed truths with more or less clearness and fulness. And this has ever been the case since Noah's time.[7]

Enough light has always been given to lead people to heaven and to punish them "if they do not employ themselves in disciplining and changing their moral nature." Thus, while Christians can claim special privileges, they do not enjoy "exclusive privileges."[8]

Arians provided an opportunity for a more extensive description of the "Dispensation of Paganism."[9] After discussing the "missionary and political character" of the Church of Alexandria and its catechetical methods, he then addresses the following question: "In what sense can it be said, that there is any connection between Paganism and Christianity so real, as to warrant the preacher of the latter to conciliate idolaters by allusion to it?" In linking Christianity with paganism, the Church of Alexandria used Paul the Apostle as a "sufficient guide" and a "full justification" for this line of instruction.[10] Newman referred to it in various ways throughout the book: "divinity of Traditionary Religion"; "divinity of paganism"; "Dispensation of Natural Religion"; and "Dispensation of Paganism."[11]

Revealed religion contains those doctrines that are taught in the Judeo-Christian dispensations and in scripture. They originate from God in a way "in which no other doctrine can be said to be from Him." Yet, on the authority of scripture itself, we are told that "all knowledge of religion" comes from God and not just that special knowledge "transmitted" by the Bible. In fact, there has never been a time when God has not spoken and told us our duty. The New Testament expressly tells us that God has never left "Himself without witness in the world, and that in every nation He accepts those who fear and obey Him":

It would seem, then, that there is something true and divinely revealed, in every religion all over the earth, overloaded, as it may be, and at times even stifled by the impieties which the corrupt will and understanding of man have incorporated with it. Such are the doctrines of the power and presence of an invisible God, of His moral law and governance, of the obligation of duty, and the certainty of a just judgment, and of reward and punishment, as eventually dispensed to individuals.[12]

Revelation is a "universal, not a local gift." The difference between Christianity and Judaism on the one hand and heathenism on the other is not the difference between who goes to heaven and who goes to hell. The point is that the "elect people of God" has always had, and the rest of humanity never did have, scripture and the sacraments as divinely appointed channels of communication. Notwithstanding, every person has had "more or less the guidance of Tradition, in addition to those internal notions of right and wrong" deposited in the conscience of every individual:

> This vague and uncertain family of religious truths, originally from God, but sojourning without the sanction of miracle, or a definite home, as pilgrims up and down the world, and discernible and separable from the corrupt legends with which they are mixed, by the spiritual mind alone, may be called the *Dispensation of Paganism* after the example of the learned Father already quoted.[13]

As well as including a patriarchal record, the book of Genesis also contains a "record of the Dispensation of Natural Religion or Paganism." For instance, the dreams of Pharaoh, Abimelech, and Nebuchadnezzar are examples of God's dealings with those "to whom He did not vouchsafe a written revelation." Job himself was a foreigner who, as a reward for "his long trial" and dogged faithfulness, heard the "voice of God out of the whirlwind." Again, the history of Balaam is about a "bad man and a heathen" who became the "oracle of true divine messages about doing justly, and loving mercy, and walking humbly." Even among the "altars of superstition, the Spirit of God vouchsafes to utter prophecy":

> Accordingly, there is nothing unreasonable in the notion, that there may have been heathen poets or sages, or sibyls again, in a certain extent divinely illuminated, and organs through whom religious and moral truth was conveyed to their countrymen; though their knowledge of the Power from whom the gift came, nay, and their perception of the gift as existing in themselves, may have been very faint or defective.[14]

While Christian missionaries believed that scripture was the "depository" of God's "unadulterated and complete revelation," they looked for points of reference in "existing superstitions" as the starting-point for catechesis. There was certainly no wholesale condemnation of "heathen opinions and practices." Nor were Gentiles treated as if they were already on the road to hell. While missionaries opposed everything "idolatrous, immoral, and profane," they believed that their task was not to uproot or reverse the existing order, but to lead people to perfection by recovering and purifying the "essential principles" of their present belief system.[15]

From this connection between Christianity and paganism, Newman drew a "number of corollaries." First of all, ridicule and satire of other religions is out of place when catechizing. While it is proper to "expose the absurdities of idol-worship," it must be done "soberly and temperately." Scoffing at an "established religion" is taboo. Such behaviour is based on the false assumption that the first step in catechesis is eradication rather than assimilation. Nobody is ever completely free of the religious system one is born into. Individuals who profess even a modicum of truth and faith are "undeniably in a better condition" to accept Christianity than the ones who deny both "human inventions, and that portion of truth which was concealed in them."[16]

Secondly, it is counter-productive to employ the doctrine of economy on "deliberate heretics and apostates." Tenderness is for Gentiles, not for those who were once "enlightened," but have since given up the faith they were baptized into. While heathen literature may not improve a person's moral stature substantially, it is still an excellent preparation for the reception of revealed truth. Heathen literature contains "scattered fragments" of truth and may be the "means of introducing a student to the Christian system," it being the "ore in which the true metal was found." Finally, the only pitfall in the Alexandrian principle is to jump to the conclusion that natural and revealed religion carry equal weight and value, "as if the Gospel had not a claim of acceptance on the conscience of all who heard it."[17]

"Dispensation of Paganism" was not without its critics. *Arians* originally began life as a history of the early Church Councils for Rivington's Theological Library series. One of the series' editors was uncomfortable about Newman's use of the term. He thought that statements about "divinely illuminated" heathen poets cast doubt on the plenary inspiration of scripture.[18]

During the Oxford Movement, Newman was often criticized for what he wrote and how he wrote. To the editor of the Evangelical *Christian Observer*, who criticized his "pugnacious," "overweening," and provocative style, he admitted that he was sometimes "militant," but denied ever being "pugnacious." There was no question of private judgment at stake here. He was doing no more than repeating what the Fathers of the Church had said about "Christ's Gospel." While he had no authority or intention of forcing his personal views on others, he "would never put it forward hesitatingly, as if I did not think all other doctrines plainly wrong."[19] In the advertisement to the first edition of *Lectures on Justification*, he reminds readers that, if they found anything "severe or contentious," or "anything else he has written," then they should "impute it to his firm belief that no wound is cured which is not thoroughly probed, and that the first step in persuasiveness is decision."[20] In the first preface to the *Lectures on the Prophetical Office of the Church*, he points out that, while his views may be somewhat controversial, his aim is eirenic, quoting John Bramhall, one of the "great" Anglican theologians:

> "My desire hath been to have Truth for my chiefest friend, and no enemy but error. If I have had any bias, it hath been my desire of peace, which our common Saviour left as a legacy to His Church, that I might live to see the re-union of Christendom, for which I will always bow the knees of my heart to the Father of our Lord Jesus Christ. It is not impossible but that this desire of unity may have produced some unwilling error of love, but certainly I am most free from the wilful love of error. In questions of an inferior nature, Christ regards a charitable intention much more than a right opinion."[21]

Once again, in *Justification*, Newman reaffirms Christ as the source of revelation. He is the "sole self-existing principle in the Christian Church, and everything else is but a portion or declaration of Him."[22] He came to "gather together in one all the elements of good dispersed through the world, to make them His own, to illuminate them with Himself, to reform and refashion them into Himself." Exactly how he "became a new commencement to things in heaven" and how he "recapitulated or ordered anew things on earth" remain a mystery:

> But this we know, that, the world being under the dominion of Satan, and truth and goodness in it being but as gems in the mine, or rather as metal in the ore, He came to elicit, to disengage, to combine, to purify, to perfect. And, further than this, He came to new-create,—to begin a new line, and construct a new kingdom on the earth: that what had as yet lain in sin, might become what it was at the first, and more than that. In His incomprehensible mercy He designed that man, instead of being a child of wrath, should be quickened and impregnated with Divine Life; and sooner than this should not be. . . . He was made man. He took on Him our nature, that in God that nature might revive and be restored; that it

might be new born, and, after being perfected on the Cross, might impart that which itself was, as an incorruptible seed, for the life of all who receive it in faith, till the end of time. Hence He is called in Scripture the Beginning of the Creation of God, the First-begotten of the dead, the First-fruits of the Resurrection.[23]

Faith is "substantially the same habit of mind" everywhere. Otherwise, it would not be called faith. Faith fulfils "two *offices*." There is the faith of the unbeliever before baptism and the faith of the justified after baptism. The former prepares the way for justification and the latter "continues and preserves" that justification. Not only does baptism enhance "all we have and all we are," it also enhances faith itself. Before the sacrament, faith is "feeble, sickly, wayward, fitful, inoperative." Potentially, it is "capable of great things, though it be nothing till Christ regenerate it." By his very presence, Christ "converts what is a condition of obtaining a favour" before baptism "into the means of holding and enjoying it" afterwards.[24]

Newman objected to liberals who thought that, while there was much "truth and value" in the early Church, it also contained contradictions, errors, and doctrines contrary to reason. For them, such teachings as the "mystical power of the Sacraments, the power of the keys, the grace of ordination, the gift of the Church, and the Apostolic Succession" possessed "very little authority." One of their guiding principles was: that, if a doctrine had traces of "Platonism, or Judaism, or Paganism," it was not, nor had it ever been, part of Christian revelation.[25] They argued that the mystical efficacy of the sacraments had its roots in Platonism, that church discipline and organization had originated from Judaism, and that ritualism had come from paganism. Since this was the case, they concluded that such things were not an authentic part of revelation. Newman disagreed. Not only do these ideas originate in Platonism, Judaism, and paganism, but "much more" comes from the "same sources." For example, traces of the Trinity, the Incarnation, and the atonement can also be found "among heathens, Jews, and philosophers." Such roots do not automatically negate their claim to be part of Christian revelation. On the contrary:

> . . . for the Almighty scattered through the world, before His Son came, vestiges and gleams of His true Religion, and collected all the separated rays together, when He set Him on His holy hill to rule the day, and the Church, as the moon, to govern the night. In the sense in which the doctrine of the Trinity is Platonic, doubtless the doctrine of mysteries generally is Platonic also. . . . Unbelievers have accused Moses of borrowing his law from the Egyptians or other Pagans; and elaborate comparisons have been instituted, on the part of believers also, by way of proving it; though even if proved, and so far as proved, it would show

nothing more than this,—that God, who gave His law to Israel absolutely and openly, had already given some portions of it to the heathen.[26]

By suggesting that the doctrine of Satan and his fallen angels was a Babylonian tenet, introduced into the Old Testament after the captivity, Michael Russell of Glasgow was, Newman thought, also suggesting that the books of the Old Testament "written after the captivity are not plenarily inspired" and, therefore, uncanonical.[27] Whether or not these doctrines were originally Babylonian was beside the point. They are still part of God's special revelation, irrespective of origin. If God could make Balaam's ass speak, God could also "instruct His Church by means of heathen Babylon"; and if God could make Peter walk on water, why could God not use a "corrupt or defective creed" as an authentic channel of divine revelation?

> It does not therefore seem to me difficult, nay, nor even unlikely, that the prophets of Israel should, in the course of God's providence, have gained new truths from the heathen, among whom those truths lay corrupted. The Church of God in every age has been, as it were, on visitation through the earth, surveying, judging, sifting, selecting, and refining all matters of thoughts and practice; detecting what was precious amid what is ruined and refuse, and putting her seal upon it. There is no reason, then, why Daniel and Zechariah should not have been taught by the instrumentality of the Chaldeans. [28]

His most important debate on the issue was with Henry Hart Milman, a leading liberal Anglican of the day.[29] In 1829 Milman had published a rather questionably orthodox *History of the Jews* treating Israel like any other nomadic tribe of the region and attaching little importance to miracles. It was criticized from the university pulpit, with one bishop going as far as to demand that it be withdrawn from circulation.[30] Newman himself singled out its "prophane spirit," calling it the "fruit of a supercilious liberalistic spirit" and the work of a "hasty thoughtless irreverent" individual who was unaware of the theological implications of his ideas.[31]

Twelve years later Milman published a *History of Christianity*, which was greeted with even more criticism and outrage.[32] Newman was furious, but reluctant to criticize it publicly because he was so depressed about the current state of the country and the future of the Church of England that, wherever he looked, he saw only gloom and doom:

> Every thing is miserable. I expect a great attack upon the Bible (indeed, I have long done so)—at the present moment indications of what is coming gather—those wretched Socialists on the one hand—then Carlile

[*sic*] on the other, a man of first rate ability, I suppose, and quite fascinating as a writer. His book on the French Revolution is most taking (to me)—I had hope he might have come round right, for it was easy to see he was not a believer, but they say that he has settled the wrong way. *His* view is that Christianity had good *in* it, or is good *as far as it goes*— which when applied to Scripture is of course a picking and choosing of its contents. Then again you have Arnold's school, such as it is (I do hope he will be frightened back) giving up the inspiration of the Old Testament or of all Scripture (I do not say Arnold himself does). Then you have Milman clinching his History of the Jews by a history of Christianity which they say is worse; and just in the same line. Then you have all your political Economists, who *cannot* accept . . . the Scripture rules about almsgiving, renunciation of wealth, self-denial, etc etc. And then your Geologists giving up part of the O.T. All these and many more spirits seen uniting and forming into something shocking.[33]

Newman was "not anxious" to draw attention to Milman's "German sources."[34] Accepting the fact that, sooner or later, biblical criticism would cause a major debate in England, he was "in no hurry to begin it." He changed his mind, however, and wrote a review for the *British Critic*, wasting no time in calling Milman's views "heretical."[35]

As with all of God's dealings with creation, Newman argued, Christianity possesses an internal and an external reality. While it may look human on the outside, it is divine within.[36] Such is the law of providence by which divine dispensations have always been conducted. The visible is both the instrument and the veil of the invisible world. It may be the veil, but it still remains the "symbol and index." Every visible item of existence and happening conceals, suggests, and reveals "events beyond itself." The "world, the Bible, the civil polity and man himself" are "representatives and organs of an unseen world truer and higher than themselves":

This is the animating principle both of the Church's ritual and of Scripture interpretation; in the latter it is the basis of the theory of the double sense; in the former it makes ceremonies and observances to be signs, seals, means, and pledges of supernatural grace. It is the mystical principle in the one, it is the sacramental in the other.[37]

The whole economy of revelation can be approached from "various, nay antagonist" points of view.[38] When divine providence reveals something, God "does not begin anew, but uses the existing system" as it is. So that, as and when God discloses facts about the Godhead, God modifies, quickens and directs the powers of nature, the laws of society or "inspires" an individual.[39] God acts "through, with, and beneath those physical, social, and moral laws" already at work.[40] Thus "addition" is the "great characteristic" of revelation. From the outside, things may look the same as before, almost as if no supernatural force is at work and life goes on as before. Looks, however, can be deceiving because behind the scenes, there is a supernatural power at work which

> . . . does not unclothe the creature, but clothes it. Men dream everywhere: it gives visions. Men journey everywhere: it sends "the Angels of God to meet them". Men may elsewhere be hospitable to their brethren: now they entertain Angels. Men carry on a work; but it is a blessing from some ancestor that is breathing on and through it unseen. A nation migrates and seizes on a country; but all along its proceedings are hallowed by prophecy, and promise, and providence beforehand, and used for religious ends afterwards. Israel was as much a political power, as man is an animal. The rites and ceremonies enjoined upon the people might be found elsewhere, but were not less divine notwithstanding. Circumcision was also practised in Egypt, frequent ablutions may be the custom of the East, the veil of Moses may have been the symbol of other rulers . . . a Holy of Holies, an altar, a sacrifice, a sacerdotal caste *in* these points the Mosaic law resembled, yet *as to* these it differed from, the nations round about.[41]

Any attempt, therefore, to treat Christianity simply as a secular institution without reference to the sacramental principle and to the sacredness of human life, is an "unreal, extravagant, and sophistical" exercise.[42] According to Newman, this is what Milman had done:

> He has been viewing the history of the Church on the side of the world. Its rise from nothing, the gradual aggrandizement of its bishops, the consolidation of its polity and government, its relation to powers of the earth, its intercourse with foreign philosophies and religions, its conflict with external and internal enemies, the mutual action for good or for evil which has been carried on between it and foreign systems, political and intellectual, its large extension, its growth and resolution into a monarchy, its temporal greatness, its gradual divisions and decay, and the natural causes which operated throughout,—these are the subjects in which he delights, to which he dedicated himself.[43]

Milman's one-sided treatment of Christianity could tempt people to conclude that what is only a "contemplation" of what lies on the surface may be mistaken for a "denial" of its divine reality.[44] Milman was actually denying that no other system is at work in this world than the "visible, political, temporal" one which we see and experience.[45] To ignore God in ecclesiastical history is to deny that God exists.[46] Although Milman cannot be held responsible for the conclusions people might draw from his principle,

Newman nevertheless takes him to task for not being aware of the "tendency of the line of thought of which both his present and a former work give such anxious evidence."

Once in the public domain, principles develop a "life and power independent of their authors," and survive in spite of them. The *History of Christianity* is an "illustration of those momentous principles" which Milman had adopted and over which he no longer had control.[47]

If left unchallenged, Milman's "External Theory" could give the impression that it had the "field" to itself, "when, in truth, there is another far more Catholic philosophy upon which the facts of the case . . . may be solved." As Newman interpreted it, this "external" theory, taken to its logical conclusion, seemed to "result or manifest itself in the following canon": "that nothing authentic belongs in the Gospel except those facts, events and doctrines which originated there. Any doctrine, therefore, claiming to belong to the Gospel, but [which] has its roots in other religions, philosophies and cultures cannot qualify as authentic Christian revelation." Newman proposed an alternative canon: "that much of authentic Christian revelation can generally be found in other religions, philosophies and cultures, either in whole or in part, and does qualify":

> . . . the doctrine of a Trinity is found both in the East and in the West; so is the ceremony of washing; so is the rite of sacrifice. The doctrine of the Divine Word is Platonic; the doctrine of the Incarnation is Indian; of a divine kingdom is Judaic; of Angels and demons is Magian; the connexion of sin with the body is Gnostic; celibacy is known to Bonze and Talapoin; a sacerdotal order is Egyptian; the idea of a new birth is Chinese and Eleusinian; belief in sacramental virtue is Pythagorean; and honours to the dead are a polytheism.[48]

Milman seemed to be inferring that because we find these doctrines in foreign cultures, they cannot be part of Christianity. Newman preferred to say that because we find these things in Christianity, they are not automatically heathen. From the beginning of time, God "has scattered the seeds of truth far and wide." Wherever they fell, they took root and sprouted up in "the wilderness, wild plants indeed but living." Though not "directly divine," all "philosophies and religions" derive their life and vitality from God:

> What man is amid the brute creation, such is the Church among the schools of the world: and as Adam gave names to the animals about him, so has the Church from the first looked round upon the earth, noting and visiting the doctrines she found there. She began in Chaldea, and then sojourned among the Canaanites, and went down into Egypt, and

thence passed into Arabia, till she rested in her own land. Next she encountered the merchants of Tyre, and the wisdom of the East country, and the luxury of Sheba. Then she was carried away to Babylon, and wandered to the schools of Greece. And wherever she went, in trouble or in triumph, still she was a living spirit, the mind and voice of the Most High; "sitting in the midst of the doctors, both hearing them and asking them questions;" claiming to herself what they said rightly, correcting their errors, supplying their defects, completing their beginnings, expanding their surmises, and thus gradually by means of them enlarging the range and refining the sense of her own teaching. So far then from her creed being of doubtful credit because it resembles foreign theologies, we even hold that one special way in which Providence has imparted divine knowledge to us has been by enabling her to draw and collect it together out of the world.[49]

The *Essay on Development* was an opportunity to focus on Christianity's perennial gift for assimilating ideas and practices from other religious systems, without sacrificing the goodness already contained in them. All religious systems possess the "same great and comprehensive subject-matter." From its inception, Christianity was surrounded by "rites, sects, and philosophies, which contemplated the same questions, advocated the same truths," and "wore the same external appearance."[50] The "cardinal distinction between Christianity and the religions and philosophies by which it was surrounded" was "that it referred all truth and revelation ... to the Supreme and Only God." Never had God left us without a witness and now, with Jesus Christ, the one Mediator, God came "not to undo the past, but to fulfil and perfect it." In spite of two thousand years of "collision and conflict," it was that Good News which succeeded in "purifying, assimilating, transmuting, and taking into itself the many-coloured beliefs, forms of worship, codes of duty, schools of thought, through which it was ever moving."[51] It is grace and truth.[52] Christianity differs from other religious systems, not in kind nor in nature, but in its characteristics, origins and in whatever the Holy Spirit has added:

> True religion is the summit and perfection of false religions; it combines in one whatever there is of good and true separately remaining in each. And in like manner the Catholic Creed is for the most part the combination of separate truths. . . . So that, in matter of fact, if a religious mind were educated in and sincerely attached to some form of heathenism or heresy, and then were brought under the light of truth, it would be drawn off from error into the truth, not by losing what it had, but by gaining what it had not, not by being unclothed, but by being "clothed upon". . . . That same principle of faith which attaches it at first to the wrong doctrine would attach it to the truth; and that portion of its

original doctrine, which was to be cast off as absolutely false, would not be directly rejected, but indirectly, *in* the reception of the truth which is its opposite. True conversion is ever of a positive, not a negative character.[53]

It is "the very nature of a true philosophy" to be "polemical, eclectic," and "unitive." By means of the continuity and firmness of her principles, Christianity has succeeded in assimilating ideas which other religious systems would find "incompatible" with their own system. The Church has never had difficulty in accepting Gnostic and Platonic ideas found in John's Gospel or acknowledging the link between the Incarnation and Platonism. She confidently adapts the "very instruments and appendages of demon-worship to an evangelical use," knowing that, if she did not utilize what she found, she would have to invent what she needed, knowing, at the same time, that she already had the archetypes on which other religions had modelled their ideas and practices. Not surprisingly, she had no hesitation in adopting, imitating, and sanctioning local rites and customs:[54]

The use of temples, and these dedicated to particular saints, and ornamented on occasions with branches of trees; incense, lamps, and candles; votive offerings on recovery from illness; holy water; asylums; holydays and seasons, use of calendars, processions, blessings on the fields; sacerdotal vestments, the tonsure, the ring in marriage, turning to the East, images at a later date, perhaps the ecclesiastical chant, and the Kyrie Eleison, are all of pagan origin, and sanctified by their adoption into the Church.[55]

Notes

1. *U.S*, p. 17, "The Influence of Natural and Revealed Religion Respectively."
2. *Ibid.*, p. 18.
3. *Ibid.*, p. 21.
4. *Ibid.*, pp. 18-9.
5. *Ibid.*, pp. 19-21.
6. *Ibid.*, pp. 27-8.
7. *L.D.* II, 281; He prefaced the 1831 memorandum as follows:"The following exposition of my own opinions, which I thought C.[Charles] ignorant of, was intended for incorporation with the above [letter]—but was omitted for want of time and space, and perhaps fortunately—for it would not profit him now, and may at some future day. The chief points which he overlooks are, that revelation is universal—and that its obscurity is intended as a trial."
8. *Ibid.*, p. 282.
9. *Ari.*, Ch. I, Sect. III, part 5, "The Dispensation of Paganism," pp. 79-89.
10. *Ibid.*, p. 79.

11. *Ibid.*, pp. 79; 73, 81.

12. *Ibid.*, pp. 79-80.

13. *Ibid.*, pp. 80-1; The "learned Father" was Clement of Alexandria.

14. *Ibid.*, pp. 81-2.

15. *Ibid.*, pp. 83-4.

16. *Ibid.*, pp. 84-5.

17. *Ibid.*, pp. 85-7.

18. *L.D.* III, 112-3. The editor was Samuel Charles Wilks (1789-1872) who was connected with the Clapham Sect. He was editor from 1816 to 1850. The full title of the book was *The Arians of the Fourth Century, their Doctrine, Temper, and Conduct, chiefly as Exhibited in the Councils of the Church, Between AD. 325, and AD. 381.*

19. *V.M.* I, 189-90.

20. *Jfc.*, p. vi.

21. *V.M.* I, xii-xiii.

22. *Jfc.*, p. 198.

23. *Ibid.*, pp. 193-4.

24. *Ibid.*, pp. 242-3.

25. *D.A.*, pp. 202-3.

26. *Ibid.*, pp. 210-1.

27. *Ibid.*, pp. 211; 213. *L.D.* VII, 32-3, Letter to Thomas Mozley (1806-93) (11 Feb. 1839). Michael Russell (1781-1848) was author of *A Connection of Sacred and Profane History, from the Death of Joshua to the Decline of the Kingdoms of Israel and Judah*, in which Newman had no objection to that statement. What he objected to was Russell's suggestion that these teachings could possibly be of human origin, without reminding people that they were also of divine origin. The reader had to make the connection.

28. *Ibid.*, pp. 211-5.

29. Milman had been Professor of Poetry at Oxford from 1821 to 1831. He was dean of St Paul's Cathedral, London, from 1849 until his death in 1868.

30. Godfrey Faussett (1780/1-1853) who denounced Froude's *Remains* from the pulpit in 1838 and singled out its editors (Newman and Keble) as dangerous members of the Church of England. An angry Newman replied in an open letter, selling over 750 copies. Newman reprinted it in *Via Media* II, 197-257. Richard Mant (1776-1848) was Bampton Lecturer for 1811, chaplain to the archbishop of Canterbury in 1813 and bishop of Killaloe and Kilfenoragh in 1820. He published a *History of the Church of Ireland* in 1840.

31. *L.D.* II, 299; 309. On 28 Oct. 1830, Newman wrote the following to his friend Simeon Lloyd Pope (1802-55) about the Milman book: "It seems to me that the great evil of M's work lies, not in the *matter of the* history, but in the prophane *spirit* in which it is written. In *most* of his positions I agree with him but abhor the irreverent scoffing Gibbon-like tone of the composition" (*ibid.*, p. 299).

32. H. H. Milman, *History of Christianity, from the Birth of Christ to the Abolition of the Roman Empire.*

33. Letter to his sister Jemima (25 Feb. 1840). Newman had just heard from John Keble (1792-1866) that socialists had set up a commune in his district where they used Sunday sermons to poke fun at the Bible. Thomas Arnold of Rugby (1795-1842) had just published two sermons on prophecy which seemed to ignore the fact that the Old Testament was an inspired document. Some of his followers said the same about the New Testament. Some political economists were equating money with morality and encouraging the rich to get richer and to ignore the poor. In addition, geologists were postulating theories about the earth's crust that seemed to cast serious doubt on the notion of a universe created in six days

and a universal flood (*L.D.* VII, 244-6).

34. 25 July Letter to H. Wilberforce (1840; *L.D.* VII, 367).

35. *Ess.* II, 203.

36. *Ibid.*, p. 188.

37. *Ibid.*, pp. 192-3.

38. *Ibid.*, p. 187.

39. *Ibid.*, p. 194.

40. *Ibid.*, p. 192.

41. *Ibid.*, pp. 194-5.

42. *Ibid.*, p. 188.

43. *Ibid.*, p. 196.

44. *Ibid.*, p. 197.

45. *Ibid.*, p. 228.

46. *Ibid.*, p. 197.

47. *Ibid.*, p. 229.

48. *Ibid.*, pp. 230-1. (1) *Magian* means "of the Magi." Magic is the science of the Magi, priests of Zoroastrianism. (2) *Gnostic* comes from the Greek word *gnosis*, meaning "knowledge"; *Gnosticism*, a religion that promises salvation via special knowledge. (3) *Pythagorean* refers to the school of the Greek philosopher, Pythagoras (sixth century B.C.). (4) *Bonze* is the European name for Buddhist monks from Japan or China. (5) *Talapoin* refers to Buddhist monks from Burma and Cambodia. (6) *Eleusinian* refers to the town of Eleusis, north-west of Athens, where the Eleusinian mysteries of Demeter were celebrated. Demeter was goddess of corn and mother of Persephone who was abducted by Hades. Demeter was so distraught that she inflicted such a disastrous drought on the land that Zeus had to intervene. It was agreed that Persephone would spend spring and summer with Demeter and the rest of the year with Hades. In the Eleusinian mysteries, we encounter a common theme in the ancient world, namely, that, "in its death and rising again to life," vegetation becomes a symbol of spiritual renewal (N. Smart, *The Religious Experience of Mankind*, p. 323.).

49. *Ibid.*, pp. 231-2. It seems highly probable that Newman had Milman's external theory in mind as he preached "The Principle of Continuity between the Jewish and Christian" on 20 Nov. 1840. In it, he asserts that all religions do not admit of "any great variety." In fact, Judaism can just as easily be charged with "Paganism for their rites, as we with Judaism for ours; for ours are not so like the Jewish, as the Jewish were like those of the Pagans" (*S.D.* p. 214; see *P.S.* V, 214-5).

50. *Dev.*, p. 355.

51. *Ibid.*, pp. 356-7.

52. *Ibid.*

53. *Ibid.*, pp. 200-1.

54. *Ibid.*, pp. 371-2.

55. *Ibid.*, p. 373. Anglo-Catholic tradition generally produces thinkers more sympathetic to the idea of universal revelation than those from an Anglo-Protestant tradition. Anglo-Catholics tend not to "isolate" the atonement from the "general process of the Incarnation." In Newman's day, Alexander Knox (1757-1831), descendant of the Scottish Reformer, and his lifelong friend Bishop John Jebb of Limerick (1775-1833) were thinking along similar lines. Knox and Jebb both believed that there are various levels of inspiration, that it exists in every age and that heathen writers were inspired as well. The more individually minded poet and theologian, Samuel Taylor Coleridge (1772-1834) was also thinking along similar lines, and so too was Frederick Denison Maurice (1805-72). Like Newman, Coleridge maintained that scripture, nature, literature, philosophy and mathematics are rich reservoirs of know-

ledge about God and God's relationship with the universe. Unlike Newman, Coleridge made no distinction between natural and revealed religion. F. D. Maurice thought that individuals everywhere and from time immemorial possess an elementary knowledge of an eternal God and that Christ is the "root and head of humanity." Although Newman's conclusions were sometimes different, his ideas were as thorough, as bold and as imaginative as theirs. See C. C. J. Webb, *Religious Thought in the Oxford Movement* (London, 1928), pp. 59-61.

CHAPTER 6

God's Message to the Heathen: Catholic Years

In his *Essay on Development*, Newman singles out a set of ideas that he calls real because they are so rich and complex in content that no proposition or number of propositions can adequately explain or exhaust their hidden potential.[1] Such was the idea of universal revelation. He kept returning to it, reminding his readers of the intimate link between nature and grace. Divine love is discernible throughout human nature by the way in which the heart is continually attracted to a greater something beyond itself, and by the way people seek solace in religion and prayer, particularly in times of crisis. Love is an indication that grace works with nature and not against it. It is "God's signature" that we are God's "property."[2] Some people are always on the lookout for divine signs and signals "under all dispensations, and in all sects," who are convinced that truth exists, "who desire to know more," who know that God alone is responsible for what they know and "who hope that He *will* teach them more."[3]

In 1851 the Irish hierarchy invited Newman to become first rector of the Catholic University of Ireland.[4] 1851 was also the year when Abbé Gaume published his controversial *Ver rongeur*, in which he argued that one of the basic causes for the de-christianization of France since the Renaissance was the use of Greek and Latin pagan classics in educating youth.[5] His solution was to ban these texts from all but the top grades in schools and replace them, in whole or in part, with early Christian writers. Gaume sent Newman a copy. In thanking him, Newman took the opportunity to say that he thought it pedagogically unsound to teach either Greek or Latin without using the classics. With the possible exception of a very select group of early Christian writers such as Athanasius and Basil, he doubted whether any of them could compete with the "simplicity, taste and grace" of a Virgil or a Homer. Just from a practical point of view, the Fathers were unsuitable material for young minds. It was part of his own world view to presume that, as Palestine "has been the seat and fountain of supernatural truth, so Attica was chosen by Providence as the home and centre of intellectual excellence."[6]

Gaume's theory was not unfamiliar to Newman. It had already been discussed in Oxford circles in the 1830s and had been aired in English Catholic circles by W. G. Ward.[7] Naturally, Newman was anxious to challenge Gaume's theory, especially as he was about to enter the field of Catholic education and as it already might find favour with the Irish hierarchy (as it did in French circles, with Cardinal Gousset and Louis Veuillot). At the time, he was preparing a series of inaugural lectures for the new university. He wrote to Archbishop Cullen sounding him out on suitable topics for the series and asked if he had seen "the good Abbé Gaume's book," commenting: "It is a startling one, to judge from a very partial inspection of it. He seems to give up Classics altogether. Is Aristotle to be given up with the rest?"[8]

His chance to defend the classics came in his third lecture as he examined theology and its relationship to other branches of knowledge. Although he did not directly attack Gaume's theory, he took the opportunity to present his own view of a universe where "all knowledge," secular and theological, "forms one whole, because its subject-matter is one," where everything is "so intimately knit together, that we cannot separate off portion from portion, and operation from operation." Even theology, the "Science of God," is not the private property of one creed or people. This "ancient, this far-spreading philosophy" can be found in classic Greece, as well as in Catholicism, Judaism, Protestantism, Russian Orthodoxy, and Islam. God is the sole source of everything everywhere that is good, true and beautiful, including pagan literature and religion. To God:

... must be ascribed the rich endowments of the intellect, the irradiation of genius, the imagination of the poet, the sagacity of the politician, the wisdom ... which now rears and decorates the Temple, now manifests itself in proverb or in parable. The old saws of nations, the majestic precepts of philosophy, the luminous maxims of law, the oracles of individual wisdom, the traditionary rules of truth, justice, and religion, even though imbedded in the corruption, or alloyed with the pride, of the world, betoken His original agency, and His long-suffering presence. Even where there is habitual rebellion against Him, or profound far-spreading social depravity, still the undercurrent, or the heroic outburst, of natural virtue, as well as the yearnings of the heart after what it has not, and its presentiment of its true remedies, are to be ascribed to the Author of all good. Anticipations or reminiscences of His glory haunt the mind of the self-sufficient sage, and of the pagan devotee; His writing is upon the wall, whether of the Indian fane, or of the porticoes of Greece. He introduces Himself, He all but concurs, according to His good pleasure, and in His selected season, in the issues of unbelief, superstition, and false worship, and He changes the character of acts by His overruling operation. He condescends, though He gives no sanction, to the altars and shrines of imposture, and He makes His own fiat the substitute for its sorceries. . . . He is with the heathen dramatist in his denunciations of injustice and tyranny, and his auguries of divine vengeance upon crime. Even on the unseemly legends of a popular mythology He casts His shadow, and is dimly discerned in the ode or the epic, as in troubled water or in fantastic dreams. All that is good, all that is true, all that is beautiful, all that is beneficent, be it great or small, be it perfect or fragmentary, natural as well as supernatural, moral as well as material, comes from Him.[9]

Newman invited T. W. Allies to lecture in the philosophy of history at the new university. Allies sought his advice on possible topics to teach. Newman suggested that the most relevant one for first year students was the "preparation of the pagan world for the coming of Christ" and that he focus particularly on Clement of Alexandria's view of pagan philosophy and the great contribution of "the four empires, the literature of Greece, and the organisation of Rome," to the early Church.[10]

His admiration for pagan classics never waned. Xenophon was one of the "best principled and most religious" writers who ever lived.[11] The Roman poet Virgil was a prophet whose very "half sentences" were "thrilling oracles" that spoke directly to the human heart. Was there anyone so solemn, so "severe in taste," and "austerely beautiful" as Sophocles? No one was more faithful to the "great laws of divine governance, providence, and immutability" than this magnificent dramatist.[12] A correspondent once asked Newman whether Platonism owed anything to Judaism.[13] It is narrow-minded and unhistorical of people, he replied, to link Plato's "glowing thoughts on the religious rites" of paganism with Judaism. Revelation is a much more universal affair. All true art, regardless of its origins, is also part of divine revelation.[14] He applauded Athenian life in the age of Pericles for the originality and sophistication of its democratic principles. To its credit, its great orators had articulated a "beautiful idea," which, though never fully realized in those golden years, would reach perfection in the eventual coming of Christ's Kingdom.[15]

Greek ethics was too close to Christian ethics to be coincidence.[16] On the matter of personal conscience, Cicero, Aeschylus, Origen, and Tertullian were "always consistent with one another." They all agreed that conscience commands, praises, blames, threatens, and suggests a future life beyond the here and now. It is more than a person's "own self." We have no power over it. We "did not make it." We "cannot destroy it," try as we may. We "can silence it." We can distort it. But we can never escape it. It will be with us to the day we die, no matter where we go or what we do.[17]

Catholics are brought up in the belief that Church and scripture are the ordinary channels of revelation, but they must not be seduced into thinking that they are the only channels. Technically speaking, when Christian theologians talk about divine revelation, they usually restrict the term to those truths which are beyond reason and contained in the Old and New Testaments. But all religion, whether rooted in nature or supernature, is part of God's mysterious plan of salvation. Divine truth comes to us in a variety of ways, including Greek poetry, philosophy, and the Koran.[18]

Of all Christians who recognized that the "*Logos spermatikos*" of classical writers was "not inconsistent with the gravity of their own literature," Newman considered Paul the Apostle as the supreme authority.[19] With Athanasius and John Chrysostom, Paul belongs to that company of saints for whom divine grace invigorated, elevated and ennobled human nature.[20] Even after his dramatic conversion on the road to Damascus, Paul went about his work like an ordinary human being, human nature having lost "none of its real freedom and power because of its subordination." The result was "that, having the nature of man so strong within him, he is able to enter into human nature, and so sympathise with it, with a gift peculiarly his own."[21] Divine grace had left him in "full possession" and control of all that was human and not sinful.[22] He knew the world so intimately and understood the human heart so profoundly that God had entrusted him with the mission of preaching the Good News to the Gentiles. Compassion was "his means of conversion," and a loving nature his power of authority.[23] His "remarkable" love for Greek literature contributed to this transformation.

Just as Moses was acquainted with the wisdom of Egypt, so Paul was acquainted with the wisdom of Greece. He loved "poor human nature," and "the literature of the Greeks was only its expression." He contemplated it "tenderly and mournfully, wishing for its regeneration and salvation," because, like Justin and Clement after him, he knew "that the Greeks were under a special dispensation of Providence, preparatory to the Gospel."[24] There is also a parallel between Paul and Philip Neri. Although Philip was no theologian, yet, by the simplicity of his life and his profound love of human nature, nobody and nothing escaped attention. Like Paul, "He lived in an age, too, when literature and art were receiving their fullest development, and commencing their benign reign over the populations of Europe, and his work was not to destroy or supersede these good gifts of God, but, in the spirit, I may say, of a Catholic University, to sanctify poetry, and history, and painting, and music, to the glory of the Giver."[25]

The final chapter of the *Grammar of Assent* focusses on natural and revealed religion. As Newman explained to an old friend, he wrote this particular chapter for ordinary Christians "who can't go into questions of the inspiration of Scripture, authenticity of books, passages in the Fathers etc. etc." and "for such ladies as are bullied by infidels and do not know how to answer them." He wanted to show that, if we keep to "broad facts of history, which every one knows and no one can doubt, there is evidence and reason enough for an honest inquirer to believe in revelation."[26]

Considering his previous statements on universal revelation, it comes as an anti-climax to find little reference to the actual topic. There are twenty pages on natural religion and eighty-four pages on revealed religion. In the section on natural religion, he simply outlines, without developing to any great length, the three principal channels by which nature furnishes us universally with a basic knowledge of God, namely, through human history, the collective mind of the human race and the individual mind. That is all. The only pagan author mentioned is Lucretius, and then only to illustrate the dark side of paganism. Christianity as the fulfillment of Judaism and the reasons for its amazing success complete the rest of the chapter.

Coming as it did in 1870, it may give the impression that he was re-aligning his theological horizons. But there had been no significant shift in his position. The reason was probably political. His letters, before and during the writing of the *Grammar*, reveal that he was anxious not to stir up a "wasp-nest" with the Sacred Congregation of Propaganda in Rome, which he once referred to as a "quasi-military power."[27] The *Rambler* affair of 1859 had raised suspicions in Rome and London that he was theologically unsound and so he preferred to remain silent.[28] This was a "great" stumbling-block to his putting pen to paper:

> This age of the Church is peculiar—in former times, primitive and medieval, there was not the extreme centralization which now is in use. If a private theologian said any thing free, another answered him. If the controversy grew, then it went to a Bishop, a theological faculty, or to some foreign University. The Holy See was but the court of ultimate appeal. *Now*, if I, as a private priest, put any thing into print, *Propaganda* answers me at once. How can I fight with such a chain on my arm? It is like the Persians driven on to fight *under the lash*.[29]

The *Grammar* was written during the heated debate on papal infallibility preceding the first Vatican Council. Ultramontanes regarded even the slightest opposition as disloyalty to Holy Mother Church. Newman made no secret about the inappropriateness of any official statement on the subject. In such a hostile climate, it is understandable that he did not want to court controversy by raising the question of universal revelation. He knew from experience how closely each new statement of his would be "malevolently scrutinized," "perverted" by "a host of ill wishers," and reported to Rome post haste.[30] Thus, he would do "more harm than good in publishing": "What influence should I have with Protestants and Infidels, if a pack of Catholic critics opened at my back fiercely, saying that this remark was illogical, that unheard of, a third realistic, a fourth, idealistic, a fifth sceptical, a sixth temerarious, or shocking to pious ears? This is the prospect which I begin to fear lies before me."[31]

To a friend, he compared the task of theologizing to dancing on a "tight rope some hundred feet above the ground. It is hard to keep from falling, and the fall is great . The questions are so subtle, the distinctions so fine, and critical eyes so many," and communication with Rome "so easy ," that you can "get into hot water before you know where you are."[32]

So concerned was he about saying anything "temerarious or dangerous" and alienating himself from the Church's official teaching, that he enlisted the services of a recognized theologian to assess the *Grammar* as he wrote it. The person he chose was Charles Meynell of Oscott College. Critical was the stage in the section of the final chapter on personal conscience and the voice of God. He told Meynell that this was so central to the book that, if he was saying anything theologically unacceptable, he would abandon the project immediately.[33] Meynell reassured him of his orthodoxy.

To quash rumours, he asked Meynell to remain silent about the project.[34] Only to friends did he confide what he was attempting, and he suggested they keep quiet.[35] Rumours, however, kept flying. One ultramontane journal had him writing a book on faith and certainty.[36] Another rumour had him hard at work on a book about rationalism which made him "very angry." He was sure that such gossip was spread deliberately by people who wanted to hinder his efforts.[37] He even left his own bishop, Ullathorne, guessing. He wrote to an old friend, Ambrose St John: "The Bishop came up yesterday and began upon my work. I said 'Oh people have been saying it these 19 years—ever since my Lectures on Anglican Difficulties—I wished I could do it' etc. etc. However, he was not taken in and changed his subject."[38]

Ullathorne was persistent and asked Newman's friends. From Rednal, Newman warned Monsell:

> Our Bishop says you have been talking to him about a projected work of mine on the Principles of Faith. By the way the Bishop spoke of it, I think he fancies it is on the question of the Infallibility of the Pope, or on

the powers of a General Council etc etc. My purpose, if I ever fulfilled it, is of quite a different kind. It is on a metaphysical question and for that reason there is a chance of my never finishing it—certainly not soon, for it requires more metaphysical and logical reading than I have. However, I mention the subject, to ask you to drop all mention of it. People are so jealous about me, that I could fancy myself quite bothered and hampered with external interference, tho' I am doing that which any one in the Church has a right to do.[39]

Newman first mentioned the *Grammar* to Ullathorne in January 1870, twelve days after writing the "last sentence" and six weeks after the Council had started.[40] It seems that Newman's reasons for not airing the topic were practical, not theological—an ironical use of the principle of reserve.[41] The evidence from the post-*Grammar* period indicates that Newman did not alter his understanding of a universal revelation. On the contrary.

A year after its appearance, he republished *Arians* and published the Milman essay (after thirty years), together with other earlier Anglican articles in *Essays Critical and Historical*. In a foreword to *Arians*, he wrote that apart from two sentences, which "needlessly" reflected on the Church of Rome and which he relegated to an appendix, no other changes had been made "affecting the opinions, sentiments, or speculations contained in the original edition."[42] Changes to the articles in *Essays* were stylistic or additional notes to certain Anglican arguments or previous statements of an "uncatholic" nature. In 1873 he republished *Tract* 85 in *Discussions and Arguments* with very few alterations. In a new preface to *Lectures on Justification*, he declared that, unless "the Author held in substance in 1874 what he published in 1838, he would not at this time be reprinting what he wrote as an Anglican."[43] He was confident that his understanding of revelation was theologically sound and could stand alongside the *Grammar*. These earlier statements really complement and enhance the final chapter.

Newman continued to reflect on revelation as a universal phenomenon whenever an opportunity arose. On being asked if the lessons learnt from the Roman poet Horace were better learnt from Thomas à Kempis, he thought that we could learn lessons from both authors. Christ certainly had a "full knowledge and love" of humanity; so too did Paul. Nevertheless:

We may gain from the classics, especially from the Latin, a great deal, in the way of that knowledge, both of man and God. The poems of Horace, I grant, are melancholy to read—but they bring before us most vividly and piteously, our state by nature, they increase in us a sense of our utter dependence and natural helplessness, they arm us against the fallacious promises of the world, especially at this day, the promises of science and literature to give us light and liberty. It is most piercingly sad to observe how the heathen writers yearn for some unknown good and higher truth and cannot find it—how Horace, in particular, tries to solace himself with the pleasures of sense, and how stern a monitor he has within him, telling him that Death is coming. Lucretius is another author teaching still more solemnly the same awful lesson. "We should be happy," he says, "were it not for that dreadful sense of Religion, which we all have, which poisons all our pleasures. I will get rid of it." But he could not and he destroyed himself.[44]

A young man once inquired to what extent the Platonic idea of pre-existence was contradictory to Christian revelation. Rather than see it as incompatible, Newman thought it a "most beautiful doctrine" and one that could be modified in a "Christian sense," rather than rejected outright. If Christians believe that "every soul has its guardian angel," is it not possible, or at least allowable, to think that a "good Angel should not whisper high truths" to children all over the world?[45]

In his 1877 preface to the third edition of the *Via Media of the Anglican Church*, he selects Paul the Apostle, John the Evangelist, and the Alexandrian Church as examples of using the principle of universal revelation as a starting point in catechesis:

> But that there is a religious way of accommodating ourselves to those among whom we live, and whom it is our duty, if possible, to convert, is plain from St. Paul's rule of life, considering he "became to the Jews as a Jew, that he may gain the Jews, and to them that were without the law, as if he were without the law, and became all things to all men that he might save all." Or what shall we say to the commencement of St. John's Gospel, in which the Evangelist may be as plausibly represented to have used the language of heathen classics with the purpose of interesting and gaining the Platonizing Jews, as the Jesuits be charged with duplicity and deceit in aiming at the conversion of the heathen in the East by an imitation of their customs. St. Paul on various occasions acts in the same spirit of economy, as did the great Missionary Church of Alexandria in the centuries which followed; its masters did but carry out, professedly, a principle of action, which they considered they found in Scripture.[46]

Matthew Arnold once delivered a lecture, entitled "A Persian Passion Play," in which he points out that Christianity brings to perfection those things we find in other religions.[47] Arnold sent Newman a copy because he felt that what he had said about Islam seemed to coincide with the ideas of the recently republished Milman essay, which he had just read. Arnold alludes to the "seriousness, elevation, and moral energy" of Mahomet, who found " . . . that scorn and hatred of idolatry, that sense of the worth and truth of righteousness, judgment, and justice, which make the real greatness of him and his Koran, and which are thus rather an independent testimony to the essential doctrines of the Old Testament, than a plagiarism from them. The world needs righteousness, and the Bible is the grand teacher of it, but for certain times and certain men Mahomet too, in his way, was a teacher of righteousness."[48] It struck Arnold that the lecture was an "unconscious" tribute to Newman.[49]

Dean Church once sent to "The Very Rev. J. H. Newman with all affectionate remembrance" a copy of two public lectures which he had recently delivered in St Paul's Cathedral. Initially, they were entitled *Civilization: Before and After Christianity*.[50] Like Newman, Church worked on the principle that ancient Greece and Rome were preparations for the gospel and, as such, part of the "*Logos spermatikos*." In thanking him, Newman said that, of all the subjects he was ever interested in, this one in particular fascinated him more than any other.[51]

One of the pioneers of study of comparative religion in nineteenth-century England was Friedrich Max Müller, one of a rare breed in those days in being both German and an Oxford professor. The university, making an exception, created a chair of Comparative Philology for him. He sent Newman a copy of his latest book, *Introduction to the Science of Religion*, the thesis of which was that all religions are different dialects of an unknown common language. Although Christian dogmas may themselves be no more than "the stammering of a child," God would "translate the faltering utterances of all his children, even those . . . we condemn because we do not understand them." In thanking him, Newman confessed that this whole area "opens upon the mind speculations wonderfully attractive and beautiful." He was in no doubt that when these dogmas eventually attained the status of scientific truth, they would bear testimony to the fact of Christian revelation.

Müller confided to Newman that the current dean of Westminster Abbey, Arthur Penrhyn Stanley, had been invited to review the book for the *Edinburgh Review*. Stanley declined on the grounds that he did not have sufficient background for discussing oriental religions. Its editor then had the bright idea of inviting Newman to review it, since he knew of nobody more capable of taking such a broad view of the subject. "I send you the message," Müller wrote, "though I feel almost certain that you will not be able to comply with this request."[52] He was right.

In an article just completed, which he sent to Newman, Lord Arundell of Wardour endeavoured to point out parallels between Latona, Mother of

Apollo, and Mary, Mother of Jesus.[53] A delighted Newman told him how grateful he was to people like himself, W. E. Gladstone, and Ignaz von Döllinger for reminding people about such "a great and important truth" as the "traditionary value" of heathen mythology in understanding Christian revelation.[54]

W. S. Lilly was secretary to the Catholic Union of England. In 1882 he also sent Newman his article on sacred books of the East, written for the July issue of the *Dublin Review*.[55] In it, he praised Newman's *Arians*, singling out his "weighty words" on the divinity of pagan religions and their link with Christianity.[56] In reply, a delighted Newman thanked him for his generous praise. Since *Arians* had been his first book, he admitted that it was "inexact in thought and incorrect in language" in places and that it needed an overhaul but that was something he was not going to do. Whatever its shortcomings, however, he had "no intention of withdrawing from the substance" of what he had written about the divinity of traditional religions. On the contrary, "I hold it as strongly as I did fifty years ago when it was written."[57]

Notes

1. *Dev.*, p. 35.

2. *S.N.*, p. 109.

3. *O.S.*, pp. 66-7.

4. The University Committee appointed Newman president of the new university on 12 Nov. 1851.

5. *Le ver rongeur des sociétés modernes, ou le paganisme dans l'éducation* ("The gnawing worm of modern society or paganism in education").

6. *L.D.* XXXI, 25*.

7. A. D. Culler, *The Imperial Intellect*, p. 264; see "The Necessities of Catholic Education," pp. 446- 57; "The Study of Classical Greek and Latin," pp. 604-14. *The Rambler*, Vol. 3 (1849).

8. Letter to Archbishop Cullen (16 Sept. 1851). *L.D.* XIV., 357-8. See Culler, *The Imperial Intellect*, p. 264.

9. *Idea*, pp. 65-6; See pp. 9; 233; 260-1; 269-70; 372. On the sixth anniversary of Newman's death, the Irish poet Aubrey de Vere (1814-1902) still remembered the "look of stern disapproval" on Newman's face as he spoke of the good Abbé's theory of education. (*The Nineteenth Century*, Sept. 1896, "Some Recollections of Cardinal Newman," p. 410). Newman appointed de Vere Professor of Political and Social Science to the Catholic University in 1855.

10. *L.D.* XVI, 244; Although Allies never took up the post, he spent virtually the rest of his life writing a series of volumes on *The Formation of Christianity*. They never achieved the breadth and comprehensiveness of Newman's less systematic views on the subject.

11. *O.S.*, p. 23.

12. *L.D.* XX, 548. In the fourth poem of his *Eclogues* (Bucolics), Virgil reflects on the common

belief of his day that a messiah was about to appear and rescue the world from its never-ending trials and tribulations.

13. Whenever Judaism and Hellenism came into cultural contact as, for example, they did in Alexandria, there was usually a circle of Jewish writers who tried to argue that Greek poets and philosophers had stolen their ideas from the Mosaic law. For example, Aristobulus (second century B.C.), an Alexandrian Jew, was one of the earliest exponents of this "theft" theory. He tried to show that, among others, Homer, Hesiod, Pythagoras, Plato, and Aristotle had stolen their ideas from an early Greek translation of the Old Testament.

14. *L.D.* XIV, 186.

15. *H.S* III, 86.

16. *T.P.* I, 138.

17. *P.N.* II, 52-6.

18. *L.D.* XXI, 121-2.

19. *H.S.* III, 60.

20. *O.S.*, pp. 92-3.

21. *Ibid.*, pp. 95-6.

22. *Ibid.*, p. 114.

23. *Ibid.*, p. 103.

24. *Ibid.*, pp. 97-8.

25. *Ibid.*, pp. 118-9.

26. *L.D.* XXV, 68. The old friend was Mary Holmes (*c.* 1815-78), one of Newman's most frequent correspondents. Newman specifically asked her opinion of the last hundred pages. See Joyce Sugg, *Ever Yours Affly, John Henry Newman and his Female Circle*, pp. 267-8. For a detailed account of Newman on natural and revealed religion, see pp. 30-1; 102-7.

27. *L.D.* XXIV, 294.

28. For a first class account of the *Rambler* affair, see Chapter 12, "The Idea of the Laity" in I. Ker's *John Henry Newman*, pp. 463-89. See also John Coulson's introduction to *On Consulting the Faithful in Matters of Doctrine*, pp. 1-49.

29. *L.D.* XX, 446-7. *Propaganda*: department of the Roman Curia, then the Sacred Congregation for the Propagation of the Faith (SCPF). Renamed the Sacred Congregation for the Evangelization of the Nations in 1967.

30. *L.D.* XXIV, 120.

31. *Ibid.*, pp. 316-7.

32. *L.D.* XXII, 215-6. Letter to Emily Bowles (1818-1904) (16 Apr. 1866).

33. *L.D.* XXIV, 297. For a detailed account of Newman on personal conscience, see pp. 48-9; 69-70; 87-8; 102-4; 118-9.

34. *Ibid.*, p. 281.

35. They included Henry Wilberforce (1807-73), Mrs William Froude, née Catherine Holdsworth (1809/10-78) and the M.P. for Limerick, William Monsell (1812-94). *Ibid.*, pp. 104; 254; 304.

36. *Ibid.*, p. 300. The journal was *The Tablet*.

37. *L.D.* XXV, 35.

38. *L.D.* XXIV, 300.

39. *Ibid.*, p. 245.

40. *L.D.* XXV, 19-20.

41. As a rule, Newman did not use the principle of reserve in his Catholic years. See R. C. Selby, *The Principle of Reserve in the Writings of John Henry Cardinal Newman*, p. 32.

42. *Ari.*, p. vi.

43. *Jfc.*, p. ix.

44. *L.D.* XXVI, 389.

45. *Ibid.*, p. 56. The young man was Edward Bellasis, junior (1852-1922) (6 Apr.1872).

46. *V.M.* I, lxxvi-lxxvii.

47. The lecture, delivered at the Birmingham and Midland Institute, was published in *Cornhill Magazine* (Dec. 1871), pp. 668-87. Arnold later included it in the third edition of *Essays in Criticism* (1888).

48. M. Arnold, *Essays in Criticism* (3d ed.), p. 260.

49. *L.D.* XXV, 440-1. See *Ess.* II, 230-1.

50. He later included them in *The Gifts of Civilisation* (London, 1880).

51. Letter to R. W. Church on 24 Mar.1872; *L.D.* XXVI, 48.

52. *L.D.* XXVI, 354-5. The editor was Henry Reeve (1813-95).

53. Published in the April issue of *The Month* and entitled "'Nigra sed formosa': An Ancient Tradition and Our Blessed Lady."

54. Letter to Lord Arundell on 17 June, 1877; *L.D.* XXVIII, 207. Gladstone published his *On the Place of Homer in Classical Education and in the Historical Enquiry* in 1857 and *Juventus Mundi: The Gods and Men of the Heroic Age of Homer* in 1876. Gladstone believed that Greek literature, philosophy, and mythology were a preparation for the gospel, and that Apollo foreshadowed Christ, Latona foreshadowed the Blessed Virgin, and Zeus, Poseidon, and Pluto collectively foreshadowed the Trinity (P. Magnus, *Gladstone: A Biography*, London, 1970, pp. 122-5; 220). The Döllinger work referred to was probably *On the Gentile and the Jew*, referred to in the *Grammar of Assent* (p. 466n).

55. "The Sacred Books of the East," *Dublin Review* (July 1882), pp. 28-32. Lilly included it as Chapter 3 in *Ancient Religion and Modern Thought* (London, 1884).

56. *Ari.*, pp. 81-6.

57. *L.D.* XXX, 105. The delicious irony of the situation would not have escaped Newman. Here was an article favourable to him and about to be published in a journal which had been highly critical of him since the *Rambler* fiasco of 1859!

PART 2

RELATED THEMES

CHAPTER 7

Revelation: External and Internal Evidences

Newman's acquaintance with the writings of William Paley dates back to 1819, when he added *Evidences of Christianity* to his personal library. Paley was recommended by Charles Lloyd in his theological seminars. Newman later recalled that Lloyd tended to make "light of the internal evidence of revealed religion, in comparison of its external proofs."[1] It is not surprising, therefore, to find Newman himself leaning toward them initially, as in the 1825 revelation sermons where he uses Paley's classical argument from design as sufficient proof for God's existence:

> We need hardly dwell on the proof presented to us in nature of the existence of a God. —When we consider the sun and stars, or turn our thoughts to the wonders of this nether world, our reason unhesitatingly declares "these things must have had a Maker"—We never should fancy a watch or other piece of mechanism came into being without a contriver—we should give no credit to, we should ridicule, we should think a man deranged, who should solemnly declare a house or ship made itself. . . . Not an hour passes, but we have renewed proof of some unseen but great author by witnessing his works.[2]

But Newman changed his mind, because he soon realized that external evidences were really "answers to objections" against revelation, rather than "direct arguments," which were "far more effective in the confutation of captious opponents" than in convincing genuine inquirers. Very few Christians had ever been converted by them, or had persevered because of any "intimate and lively perception of the force of what are technically called the Evidences." To a person with a well-informed conscience and already familiar with the truths of natural religion, the "mere fact" of Christianity is sufficient grounds for believing that a revelation, over and above natural religion, has been given. So vigilant is "the instinctive power of an educated conscience, that by some secret faculty, and without any intelligible reasoning process, it seems to detect moral truth wherever it lies hid, and feels a conviction of its own accuracy which bystanders cannot account for." This is particularly so in the case of revealed religion "which is one comprehensive moral fact."[3]

Paley belonged to that band of writers who could wax eloquent on the "order and beauty of the physical world," the "wise contrivances of visible nature," and the "benevolence of the objects proposed in them." Such notions might satisfy the "reason of the mere man of letters, or the prosperous and self-indulgent philosopher," but throw no light on God as a person.[4] They may "'declare the glory of God,' but not His will." For all their "brightness and excellence," external arguments are irrelevant to "fallen" humanity.[5] Design may teach "power, skill and goodness," but it cannot teach holiness, mercy, and the prospect of final judgment.[6] Nor does it satisfy the longings of the human heart. In fact, design tells us virtually nothing about Christianity[7]: "If I am asked to use Paley's argument for my own conversion, I say plainly I do not want to be converted by a smart syllogism; if I am asked to convert others by it, I say plainly I do not care to overcome their reason without touching their hearts. I wish to deal, not with controversialists, but with inquirers."[8]

For Newman, arguments like Paley's encouraged a passive attitude to revelation. Instead of inquiring whether further revelation has been given, some people seem to think that God owes them a favour and are quite happy to sit at home and wait for the evidence to drop into their lap.[9] He questioned Paley's premise that the credentials of revelation are of a miraculous nature.[10] The circumstances "under which a professed revelation comes to us, may be such as to impress both our reason and our imagination with a sense of its truth, even though no appeal" is necessary to "miraculous intervention."[11] The cumulation of non-miraculous coincidences overwhelmingly re-enforce the presence of God as if it were "the law of our nature."[12] Such coincidences are re-confirmation to the illative sense of those who already believe in God and "especially to those who in addition hold with me the strong antecedent probability that, in His mercy, He will thus supernaturally present Himself to our apprehension."[13]

Later, Newman preferred to focus on internal, personal evidences, whereas traditional proofs tended to rely on miracles and prophecy. He felt it was time to investigate personal proofs as this was what most people relied on.[14] Once upon a time, it was taken for granted that a person "was allowed to believe till it was logically brought home to him that he ought not to believe." As the nineteenth century gathered pace, the more common assumption was that no one should believe anything which had not been "distinctly" and rationally established beforehand. A current criticism was that religious faith, "not based upon rational grounds, is a superstition, or a prejudice, or a fanaticism, or some kind or other of unreality."[15] Most believers had neither the time nor the intellectual skill to delve into such issues—"hereditary Christians," who believed because they had been taught to believe and whose main line of defence was the "argument from authority."[16] It was for these people that Newman wrote the *Grammar*. He was convinced that ordinary Christians have quite valid reasons for believing as they do, even though they cannot fully understand and absolutely prove it.[17]

Although "the real source and cause of religious faith is beyond nature and natural reason," reason still remains its "antecedent" and "cause." If it warrants the name of faith, it must rest on reason. Just as we argue antecedently that, if a revelation be given as a revelation, it must have a prophet or an oracle, we may also argue that, if religion relies on reason, "there must be reasons producible sufficient for the rational conviction of every" man, woman, and child. The "key of the whole system is that God *desires* and imposes it as a duty" to love and serve God our Maker. If that is the case, then God "will bless imperfect proofs in religious matters," which is something not guaranteed to other sciences.[18] Since the grounds for belief apply universally, such assurances must reside "deep in the constitution of our nature." They must be "obvious and not abstract," be naturally persuasive, "intelligible," and "arrest the attention of all." Since they apply universally, they must be "portable" and require no "books or education, or an array of facts." Above all, they must be tough enough to last a lifetime.[19] Once the mind is convinced that the evidence at hand is worth believing, and common sense is convinced of this, then and only then does the "sovereign power of the will" step in and fill any gaps.[20] As the mind assents to the truth of revelation, it also realizes that, if it is going to believe at all, then it cannot do so by "halves," because "to believe in *God's word* is to believe in that which claims the *firmest* and most *absolute* assent."[21]

In proving revelation, Newman feels that he has a right to speak for himself, but for no one else. While his experiences are sufficient for him, he cannot "lay down the law" for others. All he is entitled to do is to compare his experiences with "the common stock of psychological facts." In doing so, he can be confident that, whatever satisfies him, will generally satisfy other people as well. If he "believes and is sure" that it is true, then it will, in all probability, find favour generally. This "primary evidence" is the most reliable source for believing in revelation, and it is all that people can reasonably expect from him.[22]

To trust personal and informal proofs is not to say that they cannot be formally demonstrated. While all truth ultimately rests on foundations that are "intrinsically and objectively" demonstrative, it does not necessarily follow that the "arguments producible in its favour are "unanswerable and irresistible." The "fact" of revelation may be "demonstrably true," but this does not mean that it is irresistibly true. There is a "vast distance between what it is in itself" and an individual's experience of it. Just as "light is not recognized by the blind," certain people cannot "recognise truth, from the fault, not of truth but of themselves." When people refuse to grant the assumptions asked for, it is impossible to convince or convert them, because, without assumptions of one sort or another, "no one can prove anything about anything."[23]

While "I can prove Christianity divine to my own satisfaction, I shall not be able to force it upon any one else." I might succeed if everyone reasoned from exactly the same principles. But God has made each of us different, not in the soundness of our arguments, but in those deeply personal, first principles which govern any inquiry. Accordingly, where there is "no common measure of minds," there can be "no common measure of arguments." Ultimately, proof for Christian revelation is not determined by "any scientific test," but by an inner, critical faculty Newman called the illative sense which is the "logic of good sense," the way we normally reason,[24] and the ability to make decisions without getting bogged down in detail and subjecting everything to tedious scrutiny.[25] A law unto itself, it guides our thinking far more skillfully, confidently, and accurately than any verbal reasoning.[26] It is much "too subtle and spiritual" to be scientific.[27] It is "transcendent logic."[28]

Natural religion gives us basic information about a creator God, about our responsibilities to that God, and about the prospect of future reward or punishment. Several "natural informants" supply this fundamental knowledge, including personal conscience, "popular religions," and the world we live in. The "most authoritative" and trustworthy is our own mind, "whose informations give us the rule by which we test, interpret, and correct what is presented to us for belief, whether by the universal testimony of mankind, or by the history of society and of the world."[29] Our greatest "internal teacher of religion" is individual conscience. It is a "personal guide, and I use it because I must use myself":

> I am as little able to think by any mind but my own as to breathe with another's lungs. Conscience is nearer to me than any other means of knowledge. And as it is given to me, so also is it given to others; and being carried about by every individual in his own breast, and requiring nothing besides itself, it is thus adapted for the communication to each

separately of that knowledge which is most momentous to him individually,—adapted for the use of all classes and conditions of men, for high
and low, young and old, men and women, independently of books, of
educated reasoning, of physical knowledge, or of philosophy. Conscience, too, teaches us, not only that God is, but what He is; it provides
for the mind a real image of Him, as a medium of worship; it gives us a
rule of right and wrong, as being His rule, and a code of moral duties.
Moreover, it is so constituted that, if obeyed, it becomes clearer in its
injunctions, and wider in their range, and corrects and completes the
accidental feebleness of its initial teachings. Conscience, then, considered as our guide, is fully furnished for its office.[30]

Above all, the "cardinal and distinguishing" truth which personal conscience teaches is that God rewards the good and punishes the wayward.[31]

We commonly speak of conscience as the "echo of a voice like no other
dictate in the whole of our experience."[32] A bad conscience generates
feelings of "self-reproach, poignant shame, haunting remorse, chill dismay
at the prospect of the future." By contrast, a good conscience generates
just as plainly, but less forcibly, feelings of "self-approval, inward peace,
lightness of heart and the like."[33] In every case, it is an emotional response
and "involves the recognition of a living object, towards which it is
directed."If we feel "responsibility," are "ashamed" or "frightened" at
disobeying its commands, this implies that there is:

One to whom we are responsible, before whom we are ashamed, whose
claims upon us we fear. If, on doing wrong, we feel the same tearful,
broken-hearted sorrow which overwhelms us on hurting a mother; if, on
doing right, we enjoy the same sunny serenity of mind, the same
soothing, satisfactory delight which follows on our receiving praise from
a father, we certainly have within us the image of some person, to whom
our love and veneration look, in whose smile we find our happiness, for
whom we yearn, towards whom we direct our pleadings, in whose anger
we are troubled and waste away. These feelings in us are such as require
for their exciting cause an intelligent being; we are not affectionate
towards a stone, nor do we feel shame before a horse or a dog; we have no
remorse or compunction on breaking mere human law; yet, so it is,
conscience excites all these painful emotions, confusion, foreboding,
self-condemnation; and on the other hand it sheds upon us a deep peace,
a sense of security, a resignation, and a hope, which there is no sensible,
no earthly object to elicit. . . . If the cause of these emotions does not
belong to this visible world, the Object to which his perception is
directed must be Supernatural and Divine; and thus the phenomena of
Conscience, as a dictate, avail to impress the imagination with the
picture of a Supreme Governor, a Judge, holy, just, powerful, all-seeing,

retributive, and is the creative principle of religion, as the Moral Sense is the principle of ethics.[34]

Conscience, then, is a living link between ourselves and God. By it, we take "living hold" of certain truths that God has planted in this world, though not visibly. It can state from the outset "what it takes a long argument to prove," "that good is the rule, and evil the exception," Such truths are independent of scripture, history and the Church. Conscience provides everyone with a "clear and sufficient object" of faith.[35]

Another natural informant is the various religious rites practised by people from the dawn of time. Wherever "popular" religion exists, it "has almost invariably worn its dark side outwards," and it is founded on a "vivid sense" of sin without which it "would hardly have any precepts." Its rites "proclaim or imply that man is in a degraded, servile condition, and requires expiation, reconciliation," and conversion; that there is "a realm of light and a realm of darkness" and a place of rest for the elect. Of all "rites and doctrines embodying the severe side" of natural religion, the "most remarkable" for its universality is the atonement. By performing "rites of deprecation" and "purification," people seem to say that the world they were born into is a stepping-stone to a better one.[36]

A "third natural informant" is "the system and course of the world." If this world really has a creator God, then the "established order of things ... must surely speak of His will in its broad outlines and its main issues." But, when we come to apply the principle to "things as they are," we are surprised and dismayed to find that, even "with our best efforts we can only glean from the surface of the world some faint and fragmentary views" of God. Superficially, there are but two conclusions to this "heart-piercing and reason-bewildering" phenomenon. Either "there is no creator God or He has disowned" us. Confronted with this stark choice, conscience, our "true informant," tells us that God does exist, but that we are "alienated" from that God. Thus, in one stroke, "it solves the world's mystery, and sees in that mystery a confirmation of its own original teaching."[37]

Although the "existing" relationship between God and the human race is a troubled one, "other general laws" exist to compensate.[38] One is that "religious beliefs and institutions" of any shape or form have universal acceptance. People do not normally subject themselves to the "tyranny" of religion without entertaining some hope of deliverance. The "mere hope" of future reward can lighten the load. Often, the "enjoyment" of a plentiful harvest, a loving family and caring friends are powerful reminders that God is present.[39] In the midst of trials and tribulations, people also sense that presence. The eternal hope that goodness will triumph over evil is "instinctively felt to be . . . the universal rule of God's dealings with us":

> Hence come the great proverbs, indigenous in both Christian and heathen nations, that punishment is sure, though slow, that murder will out, that treason never prospers, that pride will have a fall, that honesty is the best policy, and that curses fall on the heads of those who utter them. To the unsophisticated apprehension of the many, the successive passages of life, social or political, are so many miracles, if that is to be accounted miraculous which brings before them the immediate Divine Presence; and should it be objected that this is an illogical exercise of reason, I answer, that since it actually brings them to a right conclusion, and was intended to bring them to it, if logic finds fault with it, so much the worse for logic.[40]

There is also the universal power of personal and communal prayer providing "natural relief and solace in all trouble."[41] If revelation is God speaking to us, then prayer is us speaking to God. It alleviates the "darkness and distress which weigh upon the religions of the world." All religions are founded on the notion of an "express" revelation from gods whose wrath needs pacifying. Natural religion comes "from above." It is not the "deduction of reason, nor the joint manifesto of a multitude meeting together and pledging themselves to each other." Evidence supports the fact that the mind is so constituted as to be psychologically and spiritually geared to the notion of revelation.[42]

Another practice is "meritorious intercession." Each religion has its "eminent devotees," who live lives of prayer and penance, have access to the "Source of good," and offer blessings and protection to "their clients." While it varies from place to place and from age to age, "belief itself in the mediatorial power of the good and holy has been one and the same everywhere."[43] Inevitably, such beliefs and practices contain numerous superstitions.[44] But superstition is the "truest and best religion, before the Gospel shines" on people and far preferable to scepticism.[45] Natural religion will always be in need of completion, but, on its own, will never disclose the ultimate remedy because that constitutes the very summit of revelation, Jesus Christ.[46]

Christian revelation is both divine and carries the "evidence of its divinity."[47] While all authentic revelation comes from God, some may come "without credentials." Christianity, however, is a "definite message" from God to humanity, "distinctly conveyed by His chosen instruments, and to be received as such a message." It has to be "positively acknowledged, embraced, and maintained," not as a "probably" true message, but as one that is "absolutely" true, coming from the one "who neither can deceive nor be deceived." Nor is it a litany of propositional truths or a "philosophical view" or a "religious sentiment" or a "special morality," but a universal "authoritative teaching."[48]

Revealed religion does not and cannot "supersede or contradict" natural religion. It recognizes it and builds on it. Otherwise, it would be almost impossible to support the claims of Christianity without appealing to the beliefs people already have, because any evidence thjat rejects the "authority of that system of thought, and those courses of reasonings, out of which those evidences necessarily grew," are worthless. Belief in revealed truth presupposes belief in natural truth: "Belief is a state of mind; belief generates belief; states of mind correspond to each other; the habits of thought and the reasonings which lead us on to a higher state of belief than our present, are the very same which we already possess in connexion with the lower state. Those Jews became Christians in Apostolic times who were already what may be called crypto-Christians."[49]

Newman is adamant that he is talking to those individuals "whose minds are properly prepared for it," and who are already imbued with the "religious opinions and sentiments" of natural religion. What then are the sorts of "intellectual and moral" opinions and sentiments that constitute the "formal preparation" for entering into the evidences or proofs of Christianity? Christianity presupposes

. . . a belief and perception of the Divine Presence, a recognition of His attributes and an admiration of His Person viewed under them; a conviction of the worth of the soul and of the reality and momentousness of the unseen world, an understanding that, in proportion as we partake in our own persons of the attributes which we admire in Him, we are dear to Him; a consciousness on the contrary that we are far from exemplifying them, a consequent insight into our guilt and misery, an eager hope of reconciliation to Him, a desire to know and to love Him, and a sensitive looking-out in all that happens, whether in the course of nature or of human life, for tokens, if such there be, of His bestowing on us what we so greatly need.[50]

Christianity preaches a clear, universal message and is the custodian of a "depository of truths beyond human discovery." On it are stamped *"prima facie* signs of divinity." If Christianity does not come from God, then no revelation has "yet been given." It is nothing less than the "continuation and conclusion"of an even earlier revelation "which may be traced back into prehistoric times, till it is lost in the darkness that hangs over them."[51]

The starting point in locating "direct evidence for Christianity" has to be Judaism. Historically, Israel is known as a "people of progress," and "their line of progress is the development of religious truth." As Greece was the "home of intellectual power," Rome the home of "political and practical wisdom," so Israel was the "classical home of the religious principle." That it is a unique historical phenomenon must be of special significance. The Hebrews themselves believed their religion to be God's "direct work." They were one nation who unanimously professed as their "one distinguishing doctrine, the Divine Unity and Government of the world, and that, moreover, not only as a natural truth, but as revealed to them by that God Himself of whom they spoke." With them is the "beginning of history" and the beginning of monotheism. On this "aboriginal truth," their laws and government are "moulded," their "politics, philosophy, and literature" established, and "prophet after prophet bases his further revelations," constantly referring to a time when the Messiah would appear and bring their nation to "completion and perfection."[52]

Why then did primitive Christianity succeed beyond rational expectation? Was it, as Gibbon had suggested, a combination of Christian zeal, belief in a future life, its claim to miraculous power, its strict moral code plus its superior organization?[53]

For Newman, Christianity succeeded because Christ's disciples went into the world preaching him and converting "*in His name*." Through them, Jesus personally imprinted his image in the hearts and minds of each individual. It is that image which constitutes the principle of Christian fellowship. Thus, Jesus becomes both the "original instrument" of conversion and the sustaining principle of the moral life after conversion. He is the healer of humanity's wounds:

> When we recognize this central Image as the vivifying idea both of the Christian body and of individuals in it, then, certainly, we are able to take into account at least two of Gibbon's causes, as having, in connexion with that idea, some influence both in making converts and in strengthening them to persevere. It was the Thought of Christ, not a corporate body or a doctrine, which inspired that zeal which the historian so poorly comprehends; and it was the Thought of Christ which gave a life to the promise of that eternity, which without Him would be, in any soul, nothing short of an intolerable burden.[54]

Through the "visible symbols" of the Church and a sacramental system, Jesus continues to live in our hearts and minds as the only panacea for the human condition.

Notes

1. *A.W.* p. 71.

2. *A. S.* II. 374. Paley's conclusion was "that it was very probable that God had made further revelation; the question was whether the Scriptures, as handed down to man, constituted a true account of that revelation. He provided the evidence that it was. This included the proof of the reliability of its witnesses, of the historical authenticity of the biblical texts, of the uniqueness of the events, and of other equally salient circumstances. Acknowledging that the truth of Christianity depended on "its leading facts," Paley claimed that "we have evidence which ought to satisify us" (R. Brent, *Liberal Anglican Politics: Whiggery, Religion, and Reform. 1830-1841.* Oxford, 1987, pp. 151-2).

3. *U.S.*, pp. 65-6.

4. *U.S.*, pp. 114-5.

5. *P.S.* I, 317.

6. *L.D.* XXV, 97.

7. *Idea*, pp. 453-4.

8, *G.A.*, pp. 425-9. In arguing the case for miracles, Paley tried to prove two propositions: (1) "That there is satisfactory evidence, that many, professing to be original witnesses of the Christian miracles, passed their lives in labours, dangers, and sufferings, voluntarily undergone in attestation of the accounts which they delivered, and solely in consequence of their belief of these accounts; and that they also submitted, from the same motives, to new rules of conduct" (*Evidences of Christianity*, p. ix, 15th ed., 1814). (2) "That there is *not* satisfactory evidence, that persons pretending to be original witnesses of any other similar miracles, have acted in the same manner, in attestation of the accounts which they delivered, and solely in consequence of their belief of the truth of these accounts" (ibid., p. xii).

9. *Ibid.*, pp. 425-6. See B. Mitchell, "Newman as a Philosopher," in *Newman after a Hundred Years*, I. Ker and A. G. Hill (eds.), pp. 223-46.

10. *Ibid.*, p. 427.

11. *Ibid.*, p. 429.

12. *Ibid.*, p. 427.

13. *Ibid.*, p. 429; see pp. 343-83. For a description of the illative sense, see p. 102 of this chapter.

14. *Ibid.*, pp. 81 ff.

15. *T.P.* I, p. 84.

16. *Ibid.*, p. 85.

17. *Ibid.*, pp. 85-6. When Newman went to Rome in 1847 as a new convert, he was "terribly frightened" that his University Sermons could end up on the Index of Prohibited Books. In the end, however, he was able to show that Sermons X-XII, which set out his ideas on faith and reason were compatible with orthodox Catholic teaching. No doubt he would have been encouraged by the fact that Giovanni Perrone (1794-1876), his teacher in Rome, endorsed his views on personal, internal evidences (*L.D.* XII, 29; 32; see *L.D.* XV, 457).

18. *Ibid.*, pp. 86-7.

19. *Ibid.*, p. 87.

20. "On the Certainty of Faith," (1848), BOA B. 9. 11.

21. *L.D.* XV, 466-7.

22. *G.A.*, pp. 385-6.

23. *Ibid.*, p. 410. When it comes to "fallible" people discussing "concrete fact," Newman was "suspicious" of "scientific demonstrations." He preferred to prove Christianity in the same informal way by which he could prove the reality of life and the inevitability of death. The best

arguments are based on an "*accumulation* of various probabilities" from which "we may construct legitimate proof, sufficient for certitude." Since a loving Providence guides us, God "blesses such means of arguments" available to us. Unlike mathematics, we cannot sit around until we have strict logical proof in "concrete reasoning" and "religious enquiry." We are conscience-bound "to seek truth and to look for certainty by modes of proof, which, when reduced to the shape of formal propositions, fail to satisfy the severe requisitions of science." We have to take short cuts. Otherwise, we get nowhere (*Ibid.*, pp. 410-2).

24. *Ibid.*, pp. 412-3; 353; 358-61; 277.
25. *Ibid.*, p. 412-3.
26. *Ibid.*, pp. 361-2.
27. *Ibid.*, p. 364.
28. *Ibid.*, p. 216. For a more detailed description of the "illative sense," see T. Merrigan, *Clear Heads and Holy Hearts*, pp. 202ff.
29. *Ibid.*, p. 389.
30. *Ibid.*, pp. 389-90.
31. *Ibid.*, pp. 390-1.
32. *Ibid.*, p. 107. In explaining "how we gain an image of God and give a real assent to the proposition that He exists," we start from the principle "that we have by nature a conscience." The fact that "its promptings" may not always be "correct," should not interfere with the "force" of its "testimony that there is a right and a wrong," or with its "sanction to that testimony conveyed in the feelings which attend on right or wrong conduct." It is not an end in itself, but "vaguely reaches forward to something beyond self, and dimly discerns a sanction higher than itself for its decisions" (*Ibid.*, pp.105-7).
33. *Ibid.*, p. 108.
34. *Ibid.*, pp. 108-10.
35. *Ibid.*, pp. 117-8. See pp. 69-70.
36. *Ibid.*, pp. 392-6.
37. *Ibid.*, pp. 396-9; *Apo.*, p. 241. The "real mystery" of evil is not that it "should never have an end, but that it should ever have had a beginning." Its existence can only be explained by saying that, in addition to God's will, a hostile one also had a hand in the "disposition" of God's work, that there is a "quarrel without remedy" and a "chronic alienation" existing between God and the human race. Evil is an undeniable fact. Not only, it seems, does revelation allow it, it "*requires*" it. Apart from evil, there "need have been no revelation (*L.D.* xviii, 215).
38. *Ibid.*, p. 400.
39. *Ibid.*, p. 401.
40. *Ibid.*, pp. 402-3.
41. *Ibid.*, p. 403.
42. *Ibid.*, pp. 404-5.
43. *Ibid*, pp. 422-3.
44. *Ibid.*, pp. 422-3.
45. *U.S.*, p. 117. "Again and again He [Christ] insists on the necessity of faith; but where does He insist on the danger of superstition, an infirmity, which, taking human nature as it is, is the sure companion of faith, when vivid and earnest? Taking human nature as it is, we may surely concede a little superstition, as not the worst of evils, if it be the price of making sure of faith" (*V.M.* I, lxviii-lxix). See *Apo.*, p. 46; *P.S.* I, 320-3.
46. *G.A.*, p. 487.
47. These two characteristics are not necessarily inseparable. While all authentic revelation comes from God, some revelation may have come without credentials. For example, it is

possible that God has communicated certain truths to the human race without telling us, which God has done in certain cultures.There, "portions of revealed truth overflow and penetrate" without anyone knowing where it comes from (*Ibid.*, p. 386).

48. *Ibid.*, pp. 386-8.
49. *Ibid.*, pp. 413-4. See Epilogue, p. 151.
50. *Ibid.*, pp. 417-8.
51. *Ibid.*, pp. 430-1.
52. *Ibid.*, pp. 432-3.
53. E. Gibbon, *The Decline and Fall of the Roman Empire*, Ch. VIII (Penguin Classics, pp. 260-327).
54. *G.A.*, pp. 463-5.

CHAPTER 8

Revelation and Development

From 1816, Newman believed in a dogmatic form of Christianity expressing itself in clear doctrines (which he later came to identify with the original deposit of faith). Later, he was confident that a visible Church, equipped with sacraments conveying grace, was also an integral component of Christianity. It was implicit in scripture, and part of the early Church and the Church of England.[1] It was a principle that Protestants had ignored and Roman Catholics corrupted. Between these two extremes, he saw a middle-of-the-road Church of England, which maintained that before the Church had split into various branches, revelation could be found only in scripture, apostolical tradition and the Fathers of the Church. In spite of the initial attractiveness of the *Via Media*, he realized that it was impossible to talk about without "cutting across" Roman Catholic teaching.[2]

He had already conceded that limited development had occurred in the early Church, but was restricted to approximately the first four centuries and to the Trinity and the Incarnation. Strictly speaking, both were intellectual rather than doctrinal. The aim of intellectualizing them was to pre-empt heresy and foster "worship and obedience."[3] As it gets a better grasp of doctrine, the intellect naturally probes the central object of Christian revelation and continues to do so until it has systematized "what has all along been a principle of its affections and of its obedience." Even at the best of times, the "systematic doctrine of the Trinity should be considered as . . . a representation, economical" and "necessarily imperfect involving apparent inconsistencies and mysteries." They were given "to the Church by tradition contemporaneously with those apostolic writings, which are addressed more directly to the heart; kept in the background in the infancy of Christianity, when faith and obedience were vigorous, and brought forward at a time when, reason being disproportionately developed, and aiming at sovereignty in the province of religion, its presence became necessary to expel an usurping idol from the house of God."[4]

There is no article of the Athanasian Creed concerning the Incarnation that had not already been "anticipated in the controversy with the Gnostics." Nor any issue in Apollinarianism or Nestorianism that could not have been settled from the writings of Ignatius, Irenaeus, or Tertullian.[5] Newman went a step further in *Lectures on the Prophetical Office*, alluding to "prophetical tradition" in addition to "episcopal tradition." From apostolic times, a bishop governed his local church and protected the deposit of faith, assisted by theologians whose task was to "unfold" its mysteries, "illuminate its documents, harmonise its contents," and "apply its promises." Prophetical tradition, on the other hand, is a vast system of theological opinions, "existing primarily in the bosom of the Church," enveloping it like a cloud, ". . . at times melting away into legend and fable; partly written, partly unwritten, partly the interpretation, partly the supplement of Scripture, partly preserved in intellectual expressions, partly latent in the spirit and temper of Christians; poured to and fro in closets and upon the housetops, in liturgies, in controversial works, in obscure fragments, in sermons, in popular prejudices, in local customs."[6]

By the spring of 1839 he was at the peak of his Anglican career as a celebrated preacher and formidable controversialist. He had complete confidence in his *Via Media* theory, acknowledged a "large bold system of religion," very different from the "Protestantism of the day," and claimed as much right to hold it as Evangelicals did their doctrines, and more right than liberal Anglicans to assert theirs.[7] He was studying the christological debates of the fifth century, particularly Monophysitism, and using original texts without the assistance of secondary sources.[8] While doing so, he discovered a "*key*" to "large passages of history" previously "locked" away from him. A new pattern of events began to emerge. He started to find "every where one and the same picture, prophetic of our present state,— the Church in communion with Rome decreeing, and heretics resisting." He realized that he had been looking at the details "bit by bit" instead of trying to get a focussed view of the period. More than he was prepared to accept hitherto, he saw the pope playing a more prominent role in Church affairs. At one extreme stood Pope Julius "resisting the whole East in defence of St Athanasius," and the "Eusebians at the Great Council of Antioch resisting him" at the other extreme.[9]

Three parties emerged in the controversy: two extreme ones, the Church of Rome and a radical party of Monophysites; and, situated somewhere in the middle, a party of moderate Monophysites. He was struck by the parallel between the party in the middle and the Church of England in its attempt to steer a course between Protestantism and Rome. Until then, he believed that the Church of England as a *Via Media* institution did not have an "exact counterpart in early times."[10] History was teaching him otherwise.

Shortly afterwards, he was given Nicholas Wiseman's article on "The Anglican Claims of Apostolical Succession," drawing another parallel, this time between the Church of England and the Donatists of North Africa in Augustine's day. In condemning the latter, Augustine appealed directly to the "living present Church," whose judgment was "final" and universal.[11] The "same truth, or a parallel one," had leapt out again "in the strongest colours": namely, that in Donatism as in Monophysitism, as, indeed, in all heresies and schisms, the universal Church "is always ipso facto right."[12]

In 1841, while translating Athanasius' treatises against Arianism, he came across yet another parallel. This time, it was the Semi-Arian party, which convinced him that the "truth lay, not with the *Via Media*," but with Rome.[13] Anglican co-operation with Lutherans to create a joint bishopric of Jerusalem was a cause of despair because, if it did nothing else, "it demolished the sacredness of diocesan rights." If it was possible for England to be in Palestine, then it was equally possible that "Rome might be in England":[14] "Such has been the issue of the *Via Media*; its tendency in theory is towards latitudinarianism; its position historically is one of heresy; in the National Church it has fulfilled both its theoretical tendency and its historical position. As this simple truth was brought home to me, I felt that, if continuance in the National Church was defensible, it must be on other grounds than those of the *Via Media*."[15] Whatever "line of early history" he examined, he saw his "own Church in the heretical party, and the Roman Church in the Catholic."[16]

Around this time he was also exchanging letters with his brother Francis, who thought his ideas sounded suspiciously like the corrupt teachings of the Church of Rome. In reply to this accusation, Newman drew up his first defence of doctrinal development. Once again, a family debate acted as catalyst. He later revealed that he had been thinking about it for some time and admitted that the final University Sermon, addressing the subject, should have been number thirteen in the series, but he had delayed it "from inability or fear of not doing justice to it."[17]

Francis had accused him of subscribing to the "main principles" of Roman Catholicism for which he personally felt "so much aversion." Although not accusing his brother of endorsing papal supremacy, he did accuse him of expecting every Christian to subscribe to a creed. That was just as bad. It was like expecting everyone to kneel before "the Pope or a General Council." Evidence suggests that Church teaching was already corrupt by the end of the first century. Fourth-century Chrysostom was every inch as bad as, if not worse than, the Doctor Wisemans of the nineteenth century.[18] Either his brother should waive his demand for a definite creed or excommunicate everyone refusing to toe the line. Such a choice was "too opposed to the whole spirit of Christianity, and too odious in itself, to be justified by any quoting of texts, were there ever so great an apparatus in its favour."[19]

Responding to this charge, Newman argued that Christianity has always retained its identity. Instead of calling subsequent additions "corruptions," he preferred to see them as authentic "developments," essential for the preservation of that identity. The one, great, indubitable fact about the Church is that its "temper and principles" have been "precisely the same from first to last, from the Apostolic age to this," in spite of detractors denouncing it as "dogmatic, mystical, credulous, superstitious, bigoted, legal." Throughout the first three centuries, there was but "one, . . . large, continuous and commanding" body called the Church claiming the "exclusive dispensation of the gospel." The same Church was making the same claim two centuries later and in every subsequent century. No historical evidence exists of any other religion claiming to be Christian. Either it is Christianity or we do not know "*what* Christianity is." Although its footprints grow fainter the further we go back, they still exist "in their degree." Eventually, Christianity "vanishes in this form from the pages of history: "There is no reason why this should not be Apostolic Christianity; as it does not differ from Scripture, more than the parts of Scripture differ from each other, and does not resemble foreign systems, which came in contact with it between the first and fourth centuries, more than systems resemble each other which are acknowledged by all to be independent and distinct."[20]

Due to "external and internal causes," the Church's teaching has undergone development from the beginning—"development" meaning the "more accurate statement and the varied application of ideas from the action of the reason upon them according to new circumstances." All living systems possess an inbuilt vitality and, as they grow, they retain their original identities. The spirit of John Locke and Martin Luther has been far more influential in shaping subsequent generations than they were when alive. Christianity is no exception. Since there are no antecedent objections to the notion of development in general, there should be none to "Church developments," provided that "they harmonize with its temper and principles, are consistent with the ideas from which they profess to spring, and are professed unanimously by its members." Insofar as "these (or other) tests fail, they become doubtful."[21]

Since the fourth century "does not present greater developments upon the first" than the seventh does upon the fourth—and nobody would deny that both centuries practised the same religion—it is equally unreasonable to deny "that the fourth has the same religion as the first." From earliest Christianity, there has been a sufficient number of doctrinal developments that not only lift the taboo on the "notion of a dogmatic system," but are sufficiently developed to "furnish portions and indices of the whole system afterwards confessedly working": "Ignatius has unfolded the episcopal and sanctioned the mystical principle; from Justin downwards we have an uninterrupted testimony to the Homoüsion . . . and to baptismal regeneration; in Irenaeus, not to say in Ignatius, we find the doctrine of the Incarnation fully developed. All bear witness to the doctrine of a Trinity, and to the rule of celibacy."[22]

Newman admitted that his analysis could be "more exact." Nevertheless, he considered his explanation acceptable to people generally, "whether they submit to the religion thus ascertained or not." Once the principle of doctrinal development itself had been established, all that remained was to look at such "details" as whether the line can in every case be drawn between truth and falsehood, whether a certain doctrine was developed more or less now or then, whether this person or age agreed with that as regards it, whether all have agreed in secondary points, whether certain persons did not abuse doctrines, whether a principle has been not carried out here and there in excess, whether all ages, especially the later, have not had gross superstitions, whether corruptions have not been superadded, whether sudden crises have not hit the Church and for the instant changed the face of her profession or a panic suspended her powers of judging.[23]

No one disputes the fact that Ignatius, Clement, or Irenaeus possessed the same "narrow, severe, bitter temper and system" and the "same doctrine as is charged upon the Church now." And it would be only to that Church that he would surrender his private judgment whenever it formally spoke. Private judgment was for "accidental details" only.[24]

In his University Sermons, Newman explored the relationship between the faith of individual Christians and reason. In the fifteenth, he goes on to examine that relationship in the Church as a community of believers. He had explained that explicit, rational explanation of revealed truths is not strictly necessary for belief or a guarantee of authenticity. Just because some people cannot explain why they believe a particular revealed truth, that does not mean they do not have a "true impression" of it.[25] Likewise, in the Church, doctrines are developed over many generations through the collective mind of its members. The arduous task of systematizing is left to professionals who have time and skills to appreciate the difficulties in "developing doctrines implicitly received." Like other sciences, formal theology is "recondite in its principles" and requires "special gifts of mind for its just formation":

> Why should this class of ideas be different from all other? Principles of philosophy, physics, ethics, politics, taste, admit both of implicit reception and explicit statement; why should not the ideas, which are the secret life of the Christian, be recognized also as fixed and definite in themselves, and as capable of scientific analysis? Why should not there be that real connexion between science and its subject-matter in religion, which exists in other departments of thought?[26]

The sermon is concerned neither with the question of who is the legitimate arbiter of dogma, nor with the individual's or antiquity's role in the process, nor with infallibility. It is an attempt to account for the current Church's claim to a systematic corpus of doctrines very different from the simplicity of Christ's original teaching.

Newman thought that Anglican theology saw revealed truth as "entirely objective and detached," like Calvary or the empty tomb, with the Church in attendance in the background. Whereas Roman theology lay hidden in the "bosom of the Church as if one with her, clinging to and lost (as it were) in her embrace."[27] By the fifteenth University Sermon, his image had become the Madonna and Child.

As the universal "pattern of Faith," both in the reception and contemplation of revealed truth, Mary is not only the archetype of every Christian, she is also the model of the Church itself as she labours to understand what has been revealed and entrusted to her. She first received the revelation of the Incarnation implicitly, acted on it intuitively and reflected on its meaning for the rest of her life. At every stage, the sole object of contemplation was her son, Jesus Christ, who is the climax of revelation, past, present, and future. By demonstrating that faith is no passive substitute for the mind, Mary foreshadows the Church's active role in fathoming the extraordinary richness of the Incarnation:

> She does not think it enough to accept, she dwells upon it; not enough to possess, she uses it; not enough to assent, she develops it; not enough to submit the Reason, she reasons upon it; not indeed reasoning first, and believing afterwards, with Zacharias, yet first believing without reasoning, next from love and reverence, reasoning after believing. And thus she symbolizes to us, not only the faith of the unlearned, but of the doctors of the Church also, who have to investigate, and weigh, and define, as well as to profess the Gospel; to draw the line between truth and heresy; to anticipate or remedy the various aberrations of wrong reason; to combat pride and recklessness with their own arms; and thus to triumph over the sophist and the innovator.[28]

Catholic doctrines are not abstract propositions but a series of historical events centring on one momentous truth that "takes hold of a thousand minds by its living force."[29] Dogmatic statements elicit other aspects of the original revelation recorded in scripture and interpreted by tradition. While new doctrines continue to emanate from it, there is no question of new revelation. The resulting doctrines are corollaries of the one, complex, unified whole. They are but "symbols of a Divine fact, which, far from being compassed by these very propositions," will never be "fathomed" by a "thousand" of them.[30] In the one all-encompassing idea, every true dogma lives and breathes:

> As God is one, so the impression which he gives us of Himself is one; it is not a thing of parts; it is not a system; nor is it any thing imperfect, and needing a counterpart. It is the vision of an object. When we pray, we pray, not to an assemblage of notions, or to a creed, but to One Individual Being; and when we speak of Him we speak of a Person, not of a Law or a Manifestation. This being the case, all our attempts to delineate our impression of Him go to bring out one idea, not two or three or four; not a philosophy, but an individual idea in its separate aspects.[31]

In unfolding its infinite richness, descriptions multiply until there is a profusion of propositions. Nevertheless, we need to remember that we are dealing with a living person who is the ruling principle of all revelation. Many people select one or two propositions from the creed, claiming to possess the complete corpus of revealed truth in their hand.

He had conceded the principle of doctrinal development, but was left with two difficulties, relating to the Church of England and the Church of Rome. The Church of England was undoubtedly "separated from the great *body of Christians*" and Rome was "in *doctrine* separated from *antiquity*." For, in its Marian practices, Rome had sanctioned credal practices in "devotional forms" and encouraged them, even though they appeared nowhere in its "Creeds or Decrees of Council." As far as he could make out, Rome was wrong. It tried to justify itself by claiming the "power to reveal fresh truths," and by claiming that these additions are "not *new* truths, but developments from germs held in primitive times." This, Newman thought, was "trifling with words." All "clearsighted and honest controversialists on the side of Rome must be forced to maintain that the Church has the power of adding new truths to the Apostolic revelation. And yet this is so distinctly at variance with their own primary principles and with the Fathers that I do not see how they can."[32]

Newman wrote the *Essay on Development* immediately prior to his conversion in 1845. He wanted to explain intellectually what he was already convinced of personally—that nineteenth-century Roman Catholicism was the nearest Church to the one Athanasius belonged to in the fourth century and not a corruption of it.[33] He was convinced that Roman Catholicism was the one, true, Catholic, and apostolic Church, but he wanted to rebut the perennial criticism that it had tampered with the original deposit of faith and, in doing so, had corrupted and betrayed it. He needed to gauge his personal reaction to the evidence as it accumulated.[34] He did not write it to prove the authenticity of Roman Catholicism, but to postulate a hypothesis to answer a difficulty about its incompatibility with the early Church.[35] He wrote it for people like himself who believed that Christianity comes as a revelation with a "profession of infallibility."[36] The *Essay* differs from the final University Sermon in that its focus is Roman Catholicism, that theological development is no longer a phenomenon of the early Church, and that developments are not only "*explanations*" of the creed, they can also be doctrines.[37]

Christianity is a living, historical idea indelibly stamped on the corporate mind of the Church, an idea of such complexity and universality that it can only be absorbed bit by bit over centuries.[38] So unsystematic is scripture and so allegorical its style, that there is a compelling antecedent probability for a living, independent, infallible authority to protect the original revelation and to monitor ongoing developments.[39] These are separate operations. Revelation can occur without any evidence of divine origin anywhere, anytime, individually or universally. Science is also a "divine gift." Christianity comes with a profession and a guarantee of infallibility. All that remains is to establish the content of that revelation: "If then there are certain great truths, or proprieties, or observances, naturally and legitimately resulting from the doctrines originally professed, it is but reasonable to include these true results in the idea of the revelation itself, to consider them parts of it, and if the revelation be not only true, but guaranteed as true, to anticipate that they too will come under the privilege of that guarantee. Christianity . . . is . . . a revelation with credentials."[40]

If no external, infallible authority exists, then no revelation has yet been given.[41] As a hypothesis, infallibility "secures the object, while it gives definiteness and force to the matter" of the revelation.[42] The basis for such an authority over and above the laws governing the natural world proceeds on the analogy of nature and from the "fact of Christianity."[43] Some people might argue that the analogy of nature militates against an infallible authority.[44] But natural and revealed religion are part of the same continuum.

Revealed principles, such as mediation, are common to both nature and supernature, while revealed facts, such as the Incarnation, have no parallel to "anything in nature."[45] All religion is a matter of authority and obedience. The difference between natural and revealed religion is that the former possesses a subjective authority and the latter an objective one. Christian revelation is the "substitution of the voice of a Lawgiver for the voice of conscience." While "supremacy of conscience" is the essence of natural religion, "supremacy of Apostle, or Pope, or Church, or Bishop, is the essence of revealed." "Thus, what conscience is in the system of nature, such is the voice of Scripture, or of the Church, or of the Holy See" in revealed religion.[46]

Critics have suggested that the *Essay* opened the door to continuing revelation beyond the time of Christ and the Apostles.[47] Collectively, the evidence does not support the claim. Newman was a controversialist, not a systematic thinker. He never thought of himself as a theologian or a philosopher. In the *Essay*, as in most of his works, he uses theological and philosophical terms for immediate, practical purposes. Technical consistency was never a priority. Admittedly, it is possible to come across occasional mistakes and inconsistencies, but that does not prove he had shifted from his fundamental premise that truths implicitly known are truths already known. When we realize explicitly what we have known implicitly, we are not inventing new revelations. We are confirming our original intuitions.

When asked about new or continuing revelation, Newman categorically rejected the idea. The idea of "absolutely" new revelation is "intolerable to Catholic ears." Such a notion could never be "entertained" by anyone possessed with even the slightest knowledge of the creed or deposit: "Revelation is all in all in doctrine; the Apostles its sole depository, the inferential method its sole instrument, and ecclesiastical authority its sole sanction. The Divine Voice has spoken once for all, and the only question is about its meaning."[48] What we know about Christianity is exactly what has been revealed and "nothing more." There are just a certain number of truths revealed "directly from above" and committed to the safe-keeping of the faithful:

> From the time of the Apostles to the end of the world no strictly new truth can be added to the theological information which the Apostles were inspired to deliver. It is possible of course to make numberless deductions from the original doctrines; but, as the conclusion is ever in its premises, such deductions are not, strictly speaking, an addition; and, though experience may variously guide and modify those deduc-

tions, still, on the whole, Theology retains the severe character of a science, advancing syllogistically from premises to conclusion.[49]

Developments of the original revelation are not developments based on emotional experience. They are based on real knowledge, "partly explicit" and "partly implicit."[50] When deciding the contents of the creed or deposit of faith, both the apostles and the Church are perfect theologians using different methodologies to arrive at similar conclusions. Each is a "living treasury" of the mind of the Holy Spirit:

> The Apostles did not merely know the Apostles Creed; what knowledge could be more jejune, unless the meaning of each separate word of it was known in fullness? They must know all and more than all about the word "Son of God", which the Church has enunciated since their time. And so of every article, and portion of an article. What then is meant by the Depositum? is it a list of articles that can be numbered? no, it is a large philosophy; all parts of which are connected together, and in a certain sense correlative together, so that he who really knows one part, may be said to know all. . . . Thus the Apostles had the *fullness* of revealed knowledge, a fullness which they could as little realize to themselves, as the human mind, as such, can have all its thoughts present before it at once. They are elicited according to the occasion. A man of genius cannot go about with his genius in his hand: in an Apostle's mind great part of his knowledge is from the nature of the case latent or implicit; and taking two Apostles, St Paul and St John, according to their respective circumstances, they either may teach the same thing in common, or again what is explicit in St Paul might be latent in St John and what is explicit in St John may be latent in St Paul.[51]

Partly explicit, partly implicit knowledge was given by Christ to the *"Church with the gift of knowing its true and full meaning,"* not consisting of a "number of formulas such as a modern pedantic theologian may make theology to consist in"; but a unique "system of thought" and "a mind possessing it" can "definitely and unequivocally" decide whether a particular part of it, "as traditionally expressed," is "agreeable to, or inconsistent with" it "in whole or in part":

> I wish to hold that there is nothing which the Church has defined or shall define but what an Apostle, if asked, would have been fully able to answer and would have answered, as the Church has answered, the one answering by inspiration, the other from its gift of infallibility; and that the Church never will be able to answer, or has been able to answer, what the Apostles could not answer, e.g. whether the earth is stationary or not, or whether a republic is or is not better than a monarchy. The differences between them being that an Apostle could answer questions

at once, but the Church answers them intermittently, in times and seasons, often delaying and postponing, according as she is guided by her Divine Instructor; and secondly and on the other hand, that the Church does in fact make answers which the Apostles did not make, and in one sense did not know, though they would have known them, i.e. made present to their consciousness, and made those answers, had the questions been asked.[52]

The deposit of faith is committed to the Pope or the Church "when the Pope sits in St Peter's chair, or when a Council of Fathers and doctors is gathered round him." Only under these circumstances, is the deposit "capable of being presented to their minds with that fullness and exactness . . . with which it habitually, not occasionally, resided in the minds of the Apostles." On these occasions, the Church has a "vision" of that divine philosophy "after the manner of an intuition or an instinct." To theologians, its formal announcements may look like "deductions from the creed or formularized deposit, but in truth they are original parts of it," communicated as one unit to the Apostles and "brought to light to the minds of the Fathers of the Council, under the temporary illumination" of divine grace.[53]

Notes

1. *Apo.*, p. 49.
2. *Ibid.*, p. 104.
3. *Ari.*, pp. 145–6.
4. *Ibid.*, pp. 144–5.
5. *Ess.* I, 130.
6. *V.M.* I, 250.
7. *Apo.*, p. 93.
8. *Moz.*, II, 283. He was also in the process of editing Theodoret, Leo and Cyril of Alexandria at the time.
9. BOA Letter to Mrs William Froude (5 Apr. 1844).
10. *V.M.* I, 16.
11. *K.C.*, p. 13.
12. BOA Letter to R. I. Wilberforce (26 Jan. 1842).
13. *Apo.*, p. 139.
14. *Ibid.*, p. 149. See *Apo.*, M. Svaglic (ed.), p. 549.
15. *Diff.* I, 392.
16. BOA Letter to R. I. Wilberforce (26 Jan. 1842).
17. BOA Letter to Mrs William Froude (14 July 1844). Sermon XV is entitled "The Theory of Developments in Religious Doctrine."
18. *L.D.* VII, 319. John Chrysostom (*c*. 347–407) was Patriarch of Constantinople and later declared Doctor of the Church.
19. *Ibid.*, p. 319, Letter to Newman (29 Apr. 1840).

20. *Ibid.*, pp. 436ff.

21. *Ibid.*

22. *Ibid.*, p. 441.

23. *Ibid.*

24. *Ibid.*, pp. 441-2.

25. *U.S.*, pp. 320-1; *U.S.*, p. 254.

26. *Ibid.*, pp. 313-4.

27. *Apo.*, p. 112; Ess. I, 209-10.

28. *U.S.*, pp. 312-4.

29. *Ibid.*, p. 316.

30. *Ibid.*, p. 331-2.

31. *Ibid.*, p. 330.

32. BOA Letter to Miss Holmes (6 Sept. 1841).

33. *Dev.*, pp. 97-8.

34. As he was embarking on the project, Newman jotted down the following thoughts: "... am I in a dream? ... 5 years ... the *only* explanation for conviction strong ... either go on or go back ... middle ground impossible ... Church of Rome certainly the continuation of the Medieval Church, and not we" (BOA A. 7. 1).

35. *Dev.*, p. 30; *L.D.* XII, 332.

36. *Ibid.*, pp. 79-80.

37. BOA Letter to Mrs W. Froude (9 June 1844).

38. *Dev.*, pp. 55-6.

39. *Ibid.*, pp. 71-2; 79-80.

40. *Ibid.*, pp. 79-80. "As to what Revelation consists in, there are many things which we know on the whole, but of which we cannot tell the boundaries. I know what is morally right, yet I cannot draw a sharp line in matters of detail between what is right and what is wrong. And so there may be points in Revelation which do not positively and undeniably command my faith, while yet there are points which certainly do" (L.D. XXV, 418).

41. *Ibid.*, pp. 88-9.

42. *Ibid.*, p. 91.

43. *Ibid.*, p. 85.

44. *Ibid.*, pp. 83-4.

45. *Ibid.*, pp. 84-5.

46. *Ibid.*, p. 86.

47. Early critics included James Mozley (1813-78) and the American convert Orestes Brownson (1803-76). Modern critics include Owen Chadwick, Nicholas Lash, Paul Misner and Anthony A. Stephenson. Most of these recent objections have been capably dealt with by Ian Ker in his important essay, "Newman's Theory—Development or continuing Revelation?," in *Newman and Gladstone*, J. Bastable (ed.), pp. 145-58. See also Aidan Nichols, *From Newman to Congar*, pp. 52 ff. See also Terrence Merrigan, *Clear Heads and Holy Hearts*, pp. 90ff.; pp.263ff.

48. *Idea*, p. 223.

49. *Ibid.*, p. 441.

50. *T.P.* II, 158.

51. *Ibid.*, pp. 157-8.

52. *Ibid.*

53. *Ibid.*, pp. 159-60.

CHAPTER 9

Revelation and Mystery

While under Evangelical influence, Newman followed Thomas Erskine's example of treating revelation as a "manifestation" of religious propositions that could be systematically tabulated. At no stage did he deny the presence of mystery, but he did focus almost exclusively on those doctrines of practical effect and agreeable to reason and common sense.[1] His focus quickly altered and he began talking of revelation as manifestation *and* mystery, insisting on a reverential treatment of both.[2] Christianity is not a completely revealed system. It consists of a "number of detached and incomplete truths" belonging to a vast, as yet, unrevealed system about which we know very little.[3]

Not only is mystery an integral part of revelation, it is the "badge or emblem of orthodoxy." It is a "doctrine enunciated by inspiration, in human language, as the only possible medium of it, and suitably, according to the capacity of language." It is doctrine "*lying hid* in language." Irrespective of a person's capacity to understand, it is received in that language. According to the depth of one's faith, each revelation can be understood "more and more perfectly." It is "one and the same, independent and real, of depth unfathomable, and illimitable in its extent." Because of the mind's limitations, no revelation will ever be "complete and systematic," and in "*so far as* it is not, it is mysterious." If nothing has been revealed, then there is nothing to know, nothing to contemplate. When "something is revealed, and only something," since all has not yet been revealed, then, of its very nature, it will be honeycombed with "difficulties and perplexities":

> A Revelation is religious doctrine viewed on its illuminated side; a Mystery is the selfsame doctrine viewed on the side unilluminated. Thus Religious Truth is neither light nor darkness, but both together; it is like the dim view of a country seen in the twilight, with forms half extricated from the darkness, with broken lines, and isolated masses. Revelation, in this way of considering it, is not a revealed *system*, but consists of a number of detached and incomplete truths belonging to a vast system unrevealed, of doctrines and injunctions mysteriously connected together; that is, connected by unknown media, and bearing upon unknown portions of the system.[4]

Contrary to what Erskine suggests, there is no single leading idea or doctrine in revelation, such as the atonement, to which other revealed truths are secondary. Each one is a mystery in itself and "stands in a certain degree isolated from the rest, unsystematic, connected with the rest by unknown intermediate truths, and bearing upon subjects unknown."[5] When some truth is revealed, a "great secret" has been unveiled; though indeed a mystery.[6]

From its incomplete nature, Newman cautions us to treat revelation reverently, to avoid "all rash theorizing and systematizing," to be vigilant protecting it and to "religiously adhere to the form of words and the ordinances under which it comes to us, through which it is revealed to us, and apart from which the Revelation does not exist, there being nothing else given us by which to ascertain or enter into it."[7] The light of the gospel does not eliminate mysteries in religion. Not only do difficulties continue to be "as great as before Christ came," it actually "*increases*" them.[8] Difficulties are a test of faith. Only a humble, obedient faith recognizes revealed truth in scripture.

Scripture tells us that, through Satan, sin entered the world even though God had created the world good. Thus, evil was a mystery before God gave us his revelation, and it still remains a profound a mystery today. Revelation does not satisfy intellectual curiosity or remove doubts and difficulties, but deals with "practical knowledge" though practicality is not the measure of its authenticity.[9] Its purpose is to make us spiritual persons but not necessarily intellectual. Only by becoming better and holier persons does revelation become "light and peace to our souls."[10] No sooner do we hear the good news of eternal happiness, then we hear the bad news about eternal punishment.[11] Just as we discover "many remarkable facts" about nature by looking beneath its surface, so do we discover a "remarkable principle" when we reflect on the sublime truths of revelation: namely, "*that religious light is intellectual darkness.* As if our gracious Lord had said to us; 'Scripture does not *aim* at making mysteries, but they are as shadows brought out by the Sun of Truth. When you knew nothing of revealed light, you knew not revealed darkness. Religious truth requires that you should be told *something*, your own imperfect nature prevents your knowing *all*; and to know *something*, and not all—*partial knowledge*—must of course perplex; doctrines imperfectly revealed must be mysterious."[12]

Difficulties in revelation test "*the reality of our faith.*" To the proud and arrogant, they are "stumbling-blocks." Only the "unassuming, modest, thankful," and "obedient" appreciate revealed truth.[13] The voice of a well-formed conscience quietly "prompts us to religion," "condemns and chastises" us when we offend, assures us "that there is something higher than earth," and "incites us to a noble faith in what we cannot see."[14] If we read scripture with a humble heart and inquire with an open mind, we shall find the doctrines of the creed, even "though we may not be able to put our hands upon particular texts, and say how much of it is contained here and how much there." If we use scripture to "*prove* those doctrines, in a critical, argumentative way," then they will vanish from its pages without trace:

> We shall come to the conclusion that they are not in Scripture, and shall, perhaps, boldly call them unscriptural. Religious convictions cannot be forced; nor is Divine truth ours to summon at will. If we *determine* that we will find it out, we shall find nothing. Faith and humility are the only spells which conjure up the image of heavenly things into the letter of inspiration; and faith and humility consist, not in going about to prove, but in the outset confiding on the testimony of others. Thus afterwards on looking back, we shall find we have proved what we did not set out to prove.[15]

As long as "we act upon our belief," it does not matter "whether we believe doubtingly or not," or "know clearly or not." If we are sincere and follow our conscience, everything will follow in due course.[16]

There are aspects of Christianity "above" reason, but nothing "against" reason. If something is "against" reason, it cannot be defended because any legitimate objection raised is an "unanswerable" one. If, however, something is "above" reason, then it can be defended on the grounds that a question raised may be an "insoluble" one. Thus, the "unanswerable" objection becomes the criterion for assessing what is "against" reason, while the "insoluble" question becomes the criterion for assessing what may be "above" reason.[17] Since Christianity contains doctrines that are "above" reason, it follows that in dealing with a revelation we are dealing with many issues to which there are "insoluble" questions. For doctrines "above" reason arise from the human mind's lack of data for a solution. Human limitation "prevents solution" while it simultaneously "furnishes refutation." An appeal to human "*ignorance*" is sometimes proof that objections to mysteries are, in reality, "repellible or *untenable*." The question may be insoluble and the objection untenable.[18]

The Trinity is an illustration of a doctrine "above" reason, but not "against" it, where the question is "insoluble" and the objection "untenable." The Father is God as fully as if the Son and the Holy Spirit did not exist. The Son is just as fully God as the Father and the Holy Spirit. The same can be said of the Holy Spirit. From these statements, some could jump to the conclusion that there are three Gods. Yet Christianity insists there is but *one* God. A theologian would probably say that, in God, there are three persons of one substance; that the human mind cannot grasp the difference between "person" and "substance;" and that the two words do not really explain how, but simply "witness the fact" of the Trinity. Such an explanation is an example of repelling or demolishing an "*objection*."[19] The Trinity, Newman would say, is a truth which contains an "insoluble" question because it is "above" reason but not "against" it.[20] We should *not* begin "by saying that there are Three, and then afterwards go on to say that there is One, lest we give false notions of the nature of that One." We start by stating "that there is One God in a simple and strict sense, and then go on to speak of Three, which is the way in which the mystery was progressively revealed in Scripture."[21]

While mysteries of faith are indeed true, they are not thereby evidently true, but they require belief. The human mind which is constantly oriented to the truth assents to those things which are sufficient for belief, not just because of sufficient evidence or their intrinsic truth or a syllogism.[22] Faith is "an act of the *will*" following a "*conviction* that to believe is a *duty*." As soon as we become convinced that we "ought to believe, reason has done its part, and what is wanted for faith is, not proof, but *will*. . . . We are answerable for what we choose to believe; if we believe lightly, or if we are hard of belief, in either case we do wrong."[23]

Newman thought there to be value in identifying "just *where*" the difficulty in a mystery lies and "*in what*" way it is a mystery. Even though we shall be none the wiser for the exercise, it is good to "throw the mystery into a sentence" and give it a name. Mystery, in one sense, is not something objective but something subjective, there being nothing concrete about it. It resides in our perception and presupposes an imperfect mind contemplating a number of objective facts. When we talk about God being "incomprehensible," we do not mean that "incomprehensibility" is one of God's attributes in the same way we say that God is love because that would imply that God could not comprehend the Godhead. What we mean is that, "from the nature of the case," we cannot objectively comprehend God.[24]

No single isolated fact constitutes a mystery. Mystery lies in the "seeming incompatibility" of two or more genuine facts when juxtaposed.[25] The fact that God exists is "one of the most natural and obvious of all conceivable ideas." It is only when we put the idea of evil alongside it that a twofold problem arises. First, the existence of evil is an antecedent problem for the existence of God. Second, if we prove God's existence in spite of the problem of evil, there is a further difficulty: how can the fact of evil be compatible with this fact of a just and loving God? This "juxtaposition" of two or more "antagonist facts" creates the mystery.[26] Such too is the mystery of a triune God. The mystery resides in the "impossibility of any human intelligence" to see how propositions seeming to be "destructive" of one another can all be true simultaneously.[27] Since these "high truths" are revealed not for intellectual gratification but for spiritual enlightenment, Newman believed that mystery presents no barrier to prayer. The understanding we have of "its separate constituent propositions" is "sufficient for devotion, which lives and thrives upon single objects rather than on a collection": "The difficulty then is not in understanding each sentence of which the doctrine consists, but in its incompatibility . . . with certain of our axioms of thought indisputable in themselves, but foreign and inapplicable to a sphere of existences of which we have no experience whatever."[28]

In spite of labours, theologians can no more understand the idea of a triune God than the "dullest clodhopper." Nevertheless, they do play a role in locating and identifying the mystery. They may not understand the distinction between "God and the Word," but they can make one by employing technical jargon. The name, however, that they eventually introduce into theology remains "just as unintelligible as the truth itself is incomprehensible." While we may have gained little satisfaction by way of explanation, we can at least acknowledge the fact that it is a "recognition" by theologians "that there is a mystery." We also recognize that the name "triune God" is a "declaration *in what point* or points the mystery lies." Finally, the name "does for the mystery what the symbol x does for an unknown quantity." It allows the mind to "use it freely, to recognise it whenever it comes up again in the course of investigation, and to speak of it and discuss it with others." For instance, one of the names introduced into the doctrine of the Trinity is "person." While it does not and cannot explain the doctrine, it does express the "point of mystery."[29]

"*Person*" tells us nothing more than that the Son is the Son and is not the Father and is not the Holy Spirit. It is both the "symbol" of the mystery and the "symbol" of our "ignorance." It represents the "refutation" of an answerable objection as well as the recognition of an "insoluble" question. When we say that revealed truth involves "*contradictions*," we mean that it involves "*contrary propositions*," not "contrary doctrines." Thus the "*truths*" represented by the two propositions "that God is three and God is one," are not in collision with each other. It is merely that the two propositions themselves are.[30] Though we get little "real *satisfaction*" in locating and identifying the mystery, we have, at least, clarified some facts. It is important to know that religious mystery does exist; that, in dealing with it, there is a "call to faith"; that we have arrived at the end of the inquiry; that we have "nothing more to learn" about it as a mystery; that, although it is not an explanation, we have a "clear" idea of it; and that, in naming it, we invest it with a "sort of positive form."[31]

While the Trinity remains a profoundly sacred mystery, it *"is not proposed in Scripture as a mystery."*[32] Like the doctrine of the "One Personal God of Natural Religion," the doctrine of a triune God is notional. At the same time, however, both doctrines can also be the object of real apprehension and assent. When "really apprehended," both are capable of becoming the "object of a strong energetic adhesion," which has the power to transform people's hearts and minds. The Trinity can exert a "living mastery" over anyone, the "unlearned, the young, the busy, and the afflicted." It can hit them so forcibly as to "arrest them, penetrate them, and to support and animate them in their passage through life." Such is the "normal faith" that underpins the "spiritual life," there being nothing in the "exposition of the dogma . . . which does not address the imagination, as well as the intellect."[33]

The Athanasian Creed contains very few theological terms. Most of its language, such as "Father, Son, God, Three, One, Spirit," is concrete and "adapted" to appeal to the imagination. Before theology borrowed them, these terms were already part of the vernacular, had an "obvious and popular meaning," and were meant to retain that meaning "when introduced into the Catholic dogma." They are among the simplest words in any language. Unlike "formal theological treatises" on the topic, we do not find words such as "substance, essence, existence, form, subsistence, notion, circumincession, mystery," which are derivatives of the human mind and notional in character. The thesis that *"the doctrine of the Holy Trinity in Unity is mysterious* is indirectly an article of faith" because it is a reflection on a revealed truth, "expresses a notion, not a thing," and bears no relation to a direct understanding of the object itself. It is a "judgment of our reason upon the object":

Accordingly the mysteriousness of the doctrine is not, strictly speaking, intrinsical to it, as it is proposed to the religious apprehension, though in matter of fact a devotional mind, on perceiving that mysteriousness, will lovingly appropriate it, as involved in the divine revelation; and, as such a mind turns all thoughts which come before it to a sacred use, so will it dwell upon the Mystery of the Trinity with awe and veneration, as a truth befitting, so to say, the Immensity and Incomprehensibility of the Supreme Being.[34]

The complex whole or mystery is not the "formal object of religious apprehension and assent." Contemplated individually, each proposition is the "direct object of real or religious apprehension." The complex whole is no more than the notional object of apprehension and assent. There can be no real assent to it because, although "we can image the separate propositions, we cannot image them altogether." Mystery "transcends" human experience."[35]

Even at the best of times, we see God in "shadows." It is well-nigh impossible to bring "these shadows together, for they flit to and fro" and are never in the same place at the same time. Just as we cannot envisage the whole universe at a single glance, so is it with our "real apprehensions" of God, only more so: "We know one truth about Him and another truth,— but we cannot image both of them together; we cannot bring them before us by one act of the mind; we drop the one while we turn to take up the other. None of them are fully dwelt on and enjoyed, when they are viewed in combination.[36]

We can, however, combine our fragmented knowledge of God by an "act of the intellect, and treat them theologically." Such "theological combinations" are not "objects for the imagination to gaze upon." In the spiritual life, people become confused by the "long list of propositions which theology is obliged to draw up, by the limitations, explanations, definitions, adjustments, balancings, cautions, arbitrary prohibitions, which are imperatively required by the weakness of human thought and the imperfections of human languages." While they add little to the "luminousness and vital force with which its separate propositions come home to our imagination," such terms are necessary, not so much as a means of increasing faith, but as a bulwark against unbelief:

> Break a ray of light into its constituent colours, each is beautiful, each may be enjoyed; attempt to unite them, and perhaps you produce only a dirty white. The pure and indivisible Light is seen only by the blessed inhabitants of heaven; here we have but such faint reflections of it as its diffraction supplies; but they are sufficient for faith and devotion. Attempt to combine them into one, and you gain nothing but a mystery, which you can describe as a notion, but cannot depict as an imagination.[37]

Scripture *never* suggests that the Trinity is a mystery, for the doctrine is addressed "far more to the imagination and affections than to the intellect." Neither is it referred to as such in the Apostles' Creed, the Nicene Creed, or the Athanasian Creed. For Newman, precisely because creeds hold a special place of veneration in the liturgy, they are not just a list of abstract, theological propositions. They are acts of faith and devotion. In such a setting, it would be inappropriate to dwell on "intellectual difficulties." The Athanasian Creed, particularly, is more than a litany of theological propositions; it is a "psalm or hymn of praise, of confession, and of profound, self-prostrating homage," appealing as much to the heart as it does to the head:

> It is the war-song of faith, with which we warn first ourselves, then each other, and then all those who are within its hearing, and the hearing of the Truth, who our God is, and how we must worship Him, and how vast our responsibility will be, if we know what to believe, and yet believe not. . . . For myself, I have ever felt it as the most simple and sublime, the most devotional formulary to which Christianity has given birth, more so even than the *Veni Creator* and the *Te Deum*. Even the antithetical form of its sentences, which is a stumbling-block to so many, as seeming to force, and to exult in forcing a mystery upon recalcitrating minds, has to my apprehension, even notionally considered, a very different drift. It is intended as a check upon our reasonings, lest they rush on in one direction beyond the limits of the truth, and it turns them back into the opposite direction. Certainly it implies a glorying in the Mystery; but it is not simply a statement of the Mystery for the sake of its mysteriousness.[38]

Even in their "most elaborate" formulae, "successive definitions of the Church" observe a similar silence on the mysterious nature of the Trinity. The only places which "directly" and "almost uniformly" insist on its mysterious nature are official "catechisms and theological treatises," whose task it is to present a systematic account of it.[39] Fundamentally, there should be no conflict of interest between theology and religion. If the two did not work in tandem, there would be no solid base for Christianity. Theology is an abstract, logical discipline that endeavours to clarify and protect revealed truth. Without the support of religion, theology would be irrelevant, but good theology enters people's lives and helps them on to the God who is the object of the imagination and affections. Theology holds truth notionally in the head, whereas real faith gives real assent and real apprehension to a reality that rules both heart and imagination:

> Religion has to do with the real, and the real is the particular; theology has to do with what is notional, and the notional is the general and systematic. Hence theology has to do with the Dogma of the Holy Trinity as a whole made up of many propositions; but Religion has to do with each of those separate propositions which compose it, and lives and thrives in the contemplation of them. In them it finds the motives for devotion and faithful obedience; while theology on the other hand forms

and protects them by virtue of its function of regarding them, not merely one by one, but as a system of truth.[40]

Notes

1. BOA Sermon 123, pp. 1-3. Newman's 1825 revelation sermons reflected Thomas Erskine's suggestion that Christian revelation was a completely intelligible system with no hidden agenda and with no links to a larger unrevealed system. Ten years later, in *Tract* 73, we find Newman vigorously challenging this position. By that stage, he realized that the Erskine approach, taken to its logical conclusion, was just another form of rationalism. See T. Erskine, *Remarks on the Internal Evidences for the Truth of Revealed Religion* (Edinburgh, 1823), pp. 71-7.

2. *Ari.*, pp. 136-7.

3. *Ess.* I, 42.

4. *Ibid.*, 40-2.

5. *Ibid.*, p. 45.

6. *Ibid.*, pp. 43-4. See A. Louth, *Discerning the Mystery*, p. 144.

7. *Ibid.*, p. 47.

8. *P.S.* I, 205; 208.

9. *Ibid.*, p. 206.

10. *Ibid.*, p. 229.

11. *Ibid.*, pp. 208-9.

12. *Ibid.*, pp. 210-11.

13. *Ibid.*, pp. 211; 227.

14. *P.S.* VI, 339-40.

15. *Ibid.*, p. 340.

16. *P.S.* II, 214.

17. *P.N.* II, 101; 103. Revelation "suggests ways of seeing parallels between uncreated and created rationality, but we need not be too anxious about finding a ladder between them. God has let that down already in the Incarnation of his eternal Son within the structures of worldly being" (C. E. Gunton, *A Brief Theology of Revelation*, Edinburgh, 1995, p. 63).

18. *Ibid.*, p. 103. George Steiner once observed that "there is no construct . . . of our relations to the world, which does not include at least one hiatus in the chain of definition and demonstration. There is no mind-set in respect of consciousness and of *reality* which does not make at least one leap into the dark . . . of the unprovable" (*Real Presences*, London, 1989, p. 214).

19. *Ibid.*, pp. 103; 105.

20. *Ibid.*, p. 105.

21. *P.S.* VI, 349. One question that kept causing "great perplexity" was how to tell "whether a particular point is a mystery or not." In tackling this dilemma, Newman was responding to a commonly held opinion of the day: "that *no* objection to any revealed truth *can* be unanswerable" because "an *unanswerable objection* to a professed truth is nothing else . . . than an invincible proof that it *cannot* be true." This objection could be levelled against revealed truth either "*extrinsically*" or "*intrinsically*." First, if a particular teaching had no place in the revealed system, then the objection had to be "answerable." Otherwise, the particular teaching cannot qualify as revealed truth. Second, if a particular teaching was epistemologically and existentially untrue, irrespective of any claim to be part of an authentic revealed system, the objection would be "unanswerable" by virtue of its being an "insoluble" question, by

virtue of being "above" reason. When such a question is "insoluble," then that "truth is called a mystery" (*L.D.* XIX, 548-9; 533).

22. *Ibid.*, pp. 549-50.

23. G. H. Harper, *Cardinal Newman and William Froude, F.R.S.*, p. 77; see *Ward* II, 276-7; *L.G.*, pp. 384-5.

24. *L.D.* XIX, 532.

25. *L.D.* XXI, 235.

26. *Ibid.*, p. 236.

27. *L.D.* XIX, 532.

28. *Ath.* II, 317.

29. *L.D.* XIX, 532-3.

30. *P.N.* II, 105; 107.

31. *L.D.* XIX, 533. In any discussion of the Trinity, Newman once offered the following advice: "We may be sure that every apparent explanation is a mistake, a heresy. We must begin by confessing it unintelligible" (*S.N.*, p. 298).

32. *P.S.* I, 210; G.A., pp. 132-3.

33. *G.A.*, pp.126-7.

34. *Ibid.*, pp. 127-9.

35. *Ibid.*, pp. 129-30.

36. *Ibid.*, p. 131.

37. *Ibid.*, pp. 131-2.

38. *Ibid.*, pp. 132-4.

39. *Ibid.*, pp. 134-5.

40. *Ibid.*, p. 140.

CHAPTER 10

Revelation and Inspiration

For many Anglicans, the Bible was the sole channel of revelation, whose every word was literally inspired and infallible. Adam and Eve were historical characters. Noah built a real ark. There was a universal flood and Abraham died at the age of one hundred and seventy-five. Continental biblical scholarship posed a serious threat to such views and the threat loomed larger with the publication of *Essays and Reviews* in 1860. Some reacted critically and defensively; others went on reading their Bibles; while others, faced by the apparent disparity between scripture and the recent findings of geology and archaeology, lapsed into agnosticism.

It was Edward Hawkins who taught Newman to "anticipate that, before many years were over, there would be an attack made upon the books and the canon of Scripture." He was " brought to the same conclusion by the conversation of Mr. Blanco White, who also led me to have freer views on the subject of inspiration than were usual in the Church of England at the time."[1] White's radical ideas on the unsatisfactory nature of current theories left Newman unruffled. He already suspected that inspiration had a human and divine dimension. Anyone, he thought, who condemns revelation by its contents, runs a risk of being misled, as his brother Charles had been in 1825. The Book of Canticles may have been "erroneously" inserted in the Jewish canon, but it is a mistake to conclude that Judaism itself was erroneous. Nor was there anything in the Old Testament that could "overthrow" Christianity. There is a huge difference "between thinking the *books not inspired* or corrupted and interpolated, and the *religion false*." The New Testament is the "*record* of Christianity," it is not "*Christianity*" itself. Even if the apostles left no writings and their disciples wrote the Gospels, they would still be inspired documents, even if they contained "many misstatements." It is possible that the apostles "themselves might have written them yet with mistakes, as men commonly write." Christianity cannot be "overthrown by the detection of spuriousness or faultiness in its own professed books, much less is it by errors, granting such, in the Old Testament.[2]

In the writing of scripture, God uses each author's personality, intellect, style, and background. Yet, how human agency and inspiration cooperate in the task remains a mystery. If human error occasionally creeps in, it occurs in minor matters of fact, not in its principles.[3] If "anything is certain,

> . . . it is this,—that, though the Bible is inspired, and therefore, in one sense, written by God, yet very large portions of it, if not far the greater part of it, are written in as free and unconstrained a manner, and (apparently) with as little apparent consciousness of a supernatural dictation or restraint, on the part of His earthly instruments, as if He had had no share in the work. As God rules the will, yet the will is free,—as He rules the course of the world, yet men conduct it,—so He has inspired the Bible, yet men have written it. Whatever else is true about it, this is true, that we may speak of the history or the mode of its composition, as truly as of that of other books; we may speak of its writers having an object in view, being influenced by circumstances, being anxious, taking pains, purposely omitting or introducing matters, leaving things incomplete, or supplying what others had so left. Though the Bible be inspired, it has all such characteristics as might attach to a book uninspired,—the characteristics of dialect and style, the distinct effects of times and places, youth and age, of moral and intellectual character; and I insist on this, lest in what I am going to say, I seem to forget (what I do not forget), that in spite of its human form, it has in it the Spirit and the Mind of God.[4]

Each evangelist presents Jesus "differently." Matthew's description has a "severe sublimity," Mark's a "minuteness and exactness," Luke's a "sort of poetical beauty" and John's "heavenly and mysterious" quality is quite palpable.[5] Human language is incapable of conveying the complete portrait. Inspiration guides each of them toward this or that unfinished but authentic portrayal of him. Though the Christ of one Gospel differs in detail from the Christ of another, we can still "feed upon these representations separately" without fear of contradiction. No matter the differences, all scripture is divinely inspired. "No book is so like itself as the Bible is— yet perhaps no book is so distinct and various in its separate parts. For its writers are many, but its Light and Life is One."[6]

Following an 1840 inquiry about the inspiration of the books of the Apocrypha, Newman confessed that he was "not very well up on the Apocrypha questions," but thought, for a "variety of reasons," that Anglicans placed these books "below the line" of canonicity, having "far *more* objections to their authority" than to that of their New Testament counterparts. He apologized for not having written "very intelligibly" but offered to write again if he had muddied the waters.[7] Shortly afterwards,

Newman presented a paper on the Apocrypha and their connection with the New Testament to the Theological Society with the purpose of showing that, while the books of Apocrypha may not be strictly canonical, their texts are inspired texts.[8]

The Apocrypha form an important "connecting link" between the Law and the Gospel. While qualitatively superior to revelation outside the Judeo-Christian dispensation, they are inferior to the Old and New Testament. Nevertheless, all dispensations belong to the sacramental system. Christian revelation happened gradually and is traceable through the "course of the Old Testament history and teaching down to Malachi," only to resurface in the New Testament "in a fully developed form." There was no break in the chain of revelation or inspiration between Malachi and Christ's coming.[9] While there is very little mention of Christ's messiahship or divinity in the Apocrypha, these books do contain an important "assemblage of truths" about his Sonship which "enlarge[s] in a most remarkable way upon the characteristics and the works of Him or that which is spoken of, whether an attribute or a Person, whether a creature or a son and that in words some of which, and still more the ideas themselves, are recognized by the Apostles."[10] The "one chief peculiarity of Christianity as contrasted with Judaism" is the "spiritual promise" of an eternal kingdom rather than a temporal one. Although some "anticipations" occur in the Prophets, "no one will deny that it is much more fully insisted on in the Apocrypha." Other ideas parallelling the New Testament include the "precept of purity," the "blessedness of suffering" for truth's sake, the "special benefit of almsgiving," plus the "doctrine of a resurrection and a future life."[11] Then there are their insights into angels: while that doctrine has a "remarkable development" throughout the "latter books" of the Old Testament, it has a "still further development" in the Apocrypha, particularly in the "history of Tobit."[12]

A common criticism of the Apocrypha is that their "characteristic doctrines are drawn from heathen sources," thus disqualifying them from the chain of revelation and inspiration. Even if their origins were heathen, this factor alone would not exclude them. To say something has come into the Church from outside "is only stating the *process* by which Almighty God has taught us." The point is this: even though the "doctrine of the Divine Word or Wisdom *may* have been anticipated by the Alexandrians or Plato, and the angelic hierarchy *may* have been taught by Zoroaster," such doctrines are not restricted to the Apocrypha. Is not the platonic doctrine of the *logos* in John's Gospel and are there not angels in the book of Daniel?: "Here is another instance of what I meant to express, when I said that the common objections to the Apocrypha were inconsistent with other parts of the system into which they are introduced. They prove too much, if they could discredit the books at which they are aimed without striking at the parts of Scripture which are confessedly canonical."[13]

As an Anglican, Newman believed in the plenary inspiration of scripture, a commonly accepted view in England until a change of attitude came about in the wake of *Essays and Reviews* of 1860. By rejecting plenary inspiration, its authors raised the issue of the Bible's historical veracity as the revealed word of God.[14] His early attitude to the new wave of biblical criticism had been cautious, alerted, perhaps, to its shortcomings by Pusey, who was having second thoughts about the value of the studies undertaken in Germany in 1826-7. Newman himself was not opposed to theologians studying foreign languages, archaeology, geology, or hermeneutics, but disapproved of the over-rigorous application of new principles to religion in general and to scripture in particular.[15] His reservations later mellowed, but he still thought that theologians needed time to be properly trained in modern methods of biblical criticism.[16] As a Roman Catholic he was understandably hesitant about his own part in it and wary of negative reaction to any comment he was likely to make: "All these German theories will come before us and have to be answered. The answer requires a great deal of previous discussion, and Catholics must first learn many controversial principles and facts, which at present they shrink from. If I begin to attack the German school, I should at once be attacked in my rear by some narrow-minded disputant of our own Creed. This is the difficulty of our position, and time alone will overcome it."[17] The years brought increased maturity to his attitude toward science and religion. Since becoming a Roman Catholic, he no longer felt the weight of past difficulties, but that did not mean that he or anyone could afford the luxury of ignoring the questions being posed by a Darwin or a Huxley.[18]

He wanted to avoid "any collision" between scripture and science "as regards the statements of the written Word." Contrary to what some people thought, science posed no threat to Christianity or Scripture.[19] Nature and revelation are "two separate communications from the same Infinite Truth!"[20] Provided that "each party will but consent to remain within its own boundaries," scripture and science could be compatible.[21] There should be no anxiety about the "free exercise" of reason in science because it is really the "minister of faith." Occasionally, it oversteps the boundary and has to be put in its place like "some of those old, true, and really good . . . servants, who take liberties, are rude, both in act and speech, sometimes disobey and take their own course, but still are never gone from home for any long time."[22] When difficulties arise, the worst thing is to panic, because that will give the impression that scripture and science are indeed irreconcilable, which they are not. It is best to sort out the difficulty calmly, always submitting to the Church whenever it speaks authoritatively on any issue.[23]

The publication of *Essays and Reviews* was a watershed in English theology. Its contributors criticized the old-fashioned methods of English theology and the "complacent ignorance" surrounding it.[24] They advocated freer theological discussion and new tools of research. Until plenary inspiration had been reconsidered, the gulf between the Establishment and its intelligentsia would widen. Newman had no disagreement with their notions of a universal revelation and of a human and divine dimension to scripture. He would, however, have disagreed with Baden Powell's treatment of miracles and Wilson's rejection of the dogmatic principle and of a divinely appointed infallible interpreter of scripture.[25] For him, plenary inspiration was "peculiarly" a Protestant problem. While Catholics believe, as Protestants do, that scripture is the revealed word of God, they do so on the authority of a Church whom they acknowledge as its official interpreter.[26] Apart from saying which books belonged to the canon and that its writers were inspired, Rome had left the question open, thereby allowing more freedom of opinion on the subject than on others.[27]

In the wake of *Essays and Reviews*, Newman undertook a study of inspiration with a view to publishing a book.[28] It never materialized.[29] In addressing the issue, he wanted to clarify the Church's teaching on the fact, the nature, and the extent of inspiration. His first acquaintance with Roman Catholic teaching on inspiration came through Perrone's *Praelectiones Theologicae* and he was surprised to find that, apart from settling the canon of scripture, the inspiration of its authors and God's authorship, little had been said on the subject.[30] Perrone criticized the theory of divine dictation, warned against a minimalist approach and pointed out that inspiration referred more to the ideas than to actual words and phrases. Facts from other sources do not have to be divinely revealed. It was enough that God's presence is manifest throughout. Sometimes, inspiration comes in the form of negative support.[31]

The sacramental principle is an essential aspect of inspiration as it is of the Church and its liturgy and, indeed, of the process of revelation itself. In the writing, God utilizes the unique talent, temperament, and background of each author:[32] "An inspired Prophet exists before his inspiration; he is a man as other men; he has a human mind, human thoughts, human knowledge. Inspiration does not create, does not destroy his human nature; it adds to it. It raises him in religious thought and knowledge above himself. He is breathed into and filled with a power greater than what nature has given him; but nature is still there."[33]

If the chosen instrument lacks a skill, God supplies the shortfall in the form of illumination, "superintendence," direct manifestation, impulse to write, "dictation," "quasi-dictation."[34] Inspiration is whatever method God chooses to get a particular task completed:

> Taking for granted then [that] the Scriptures were the work of inspired men, writing under inspiration, what was it that we are to suppose in consequence that this gift did for their minds and their pens as they wrote? I suppose the direct answer to this question is, that the gift answered their needs, was equal to their wants, whatever in each particular case it might be; if illumination as to doctrine was wanted, it was the gift of illumination; if prudence in selecting or rejecting matter, it was prudence; if the power of prophesying, it was foreknowledge; if the knowledge of facts, historical accuracy; if faculty of expression, the use of language. First, it illuminated them generally, vivified their memory, and raised their minds in knowledge and comprehension above the very subject-matter which was to be the substance of their writing; so that they might be said to master it, in such a sense that they could have said much more upon it than they were led to say, saw its connection with other subjects, and were in consequence fit recipients of the further gift of . . . prudence; by which they selected the points to be treated, or incidents to be mentioned, and used the exact words suitably to express their meaning, in order to subserve the great ends which were . . . put before them as the scope of their writing at all.[35]

Revelation and inspiration are not synonymous. Inspiration presupposes the fact of revelation. Revelation is about what is revealed, inspiration about how it is revealed. It is a process of transmitting to each author the word of God "without addition or diminution." Infallibility is the "end and the effect of inspiration" and "supplemental" to the act of revelation itself. It is "that spiritual endowment, whereby the recipients of a revelation" become channels of revealed truth, "whether by word or by deed."[36]

If an author is inspired, it should follow that the book is also inspired. While the Bible may look like other books, it is intrinsically different. While there is no insurmountable difficulty understanding that an author is inspired, there is a difficulty when we say "that words and letters, written with a pen, inscribed upon wax, or printed by types, have in them a secret divine gift, and are different from other words, spoken by whomsoever." Is it enough to say that a book is inspired because of some mysterious power and stop there? If we say it is inspired, then there has to be some supernatural "intrinsic gift" determining and informing the books. Inspiration of the sacred writers is not a permanent gift, but inspiration of sacred texts is. How then do we explain this unique phenomenon that mysteriously transforms a writer's words into a divine message?[37]

First, there is the dictation theory. which says that the words of the text are "actually dictated by Almighty God." This is the "highest view which can be taken of their sacred character." The weakness of this theory is that, while dictation enhances the "sacredness of Scripture, . . . it lowers the dignity of the inspired writer, who becomes a mere instrument or organ" in the process. Dictation is not inspiration:

> In everyday matters of the world, we tell of a man's dictating a letter; in that case he does everything but use his own hand. On the contrary, we speak of a journal, or review, being written under the inspirations of the ministry [government] or some political party; by this we mean that as far as the purposes of government or of the particular party are concerned, the spirit breathed into it, the spirit it breathes, is conservative, or liberal, or progressive, or the like as the case may be. Portions of such a journal . . . indeed may actually be dictated by the persons whose organ it is; but, looking at it as a whole, as an existing publication which, without ceasing to give the general news of the world, law intelligence, commercial intelligence and whatever a newspaper contains, is, over and above all this, the channel . . . and advocate of Whig measures or Tory measures, we should say it was under the inspiration of this or that political party. I am using this illustration, not as a sufficient description of what inspiration is, but in order to mark the difference between dictation and inspiration.[38]

Dictation involves the "substance" of scripture, while "inspiration implies a quality of it." When we say that certain individuals were inspired, we mean that "their minds were exalted, enlarged and purified, intellectually and morally." When we say that a book is inspired, "we mean that a human composition is made the vehicle of a divine message." Dictation requires only the "co-operation of the human will," while "inspiration presupposes the operation of the human intellect." Inspiration admits of degree, dictation does not. Dictation "has one sense only." Inspiration has many.[39]

Second, there is the theory of inerrancy, which says, "when Scripture is said to be inspired, the intrinsic gift which is denoted as supernaturally imparted, is that it is absolutely and in all matters the Truth." As dictation is the "highest view" of inspiration, inerrancy is the "lowest." While truth and exactitude may be the "object" of inspiration and the "effect of the gift," they are not "that in which the gift consists." For example, the writings of Gregory Nazianzen "are said to be free in all parts from any error," yet people do not normally refer to them as inspired documents. As "dictation expresses one idea and inspiration another," so is it "one thing to be inspired, and another thing to be true." As "dictation is more than inspiration, so it would seem that exactitude is less."[40]

Third, there is the idea that inspiration lies in "its quasi-sacramental power." Scripture may possess a "force, an influence, and an operation, which is simply supernatural," but there are "other writings and other preachings and discourses" that have had similar effects on people. If the "power of touching the heart, converting the sinful, consoling the troubled or instructing the devout are to be the criterion of inspiration, has not the *Imitation of Christ* more claims to be considered an inspired work than the Book of Esther or the second book of Maccabees?"[41]

Finally, there is the theory of verbal inspiration which Newman thought was "perhaps the most satisfactory account of it." Verbal inspiration consists in "heavenly doctrine, instruction, warning, or consolation, such as a man could not give," and "which is conveyed through the words of Moses or Jeremias, Paul, or John." When "Scripture is emphatically called 'the Word of God,' it is considered surely in that sense in which God spoke it," and not in the way an individual speaks it. When viewed in "that divine sense," then every "sentence" of a sacred text becomes God's word. Although parts of it may once have been "the word of man," God has, "as it were, spoken the whole of it over again and made it His even in those human parts by the new sense or drift which He has put into them." Hence, it is the unique "presence of this divine authoritative voice in Scripture, as it is in no other writings, which constitutes its inspiration."[42]

Catholics had been saved the onerous, if not impossible, task of ascertaining its inspired meaning because the Church itself is "its divinely appointed . . . interpreter in that divine authoritative sense." There is no "more important and necessary truth" than this. Though infallible statements on particular passages and texts are rare and follow only after a "long course of controversies," it reserves the right to reject interpretations running "counter to the unanimous consent of the Fathers": "But as to the Scriptures in their length and breadth, that meaning which is inspired has never yet been determined, and still remains in the bosom of the Church. The comments of great doctors, though vested with great 'authority,' are still human; they are not the voice of the Infallible God. The adaptations of mystical writings are most important for the purposes of meditation and devotion; but they are no guide to the exegetical theologian."[43]

Grammatically, inspiration has an "active" and a "passive" meaning. In its active sense, it refers to a "prompting to act, to speak or to write," originating from God. In its passive sense, it refers to a person or book being inspired, permanently or temporarily.[44] "Prophets, Apostles, Evangelists" had permanent inspiration. While everything they did and said excited the "interest and veneration" of people, not everything was of "equal" value or interest. There would have been more opportunity for inspiration when talking about salvation than about "their native country, their citizenship, the hour of the day, and the length of a journey." But we should still listen with "faith and awe" to whatever is said.[45]

In 1884 Newman published an essay on "Inspiration in its Relation to Revelation," to "state what we really do hold as regards Holy Scripture, and what a Catholic is bound to believe."[46] The Church teaches that scripture is "divinely inspired throughout" in matters of faith and morals, and that it alone is "the one infallible expounder of that inspired text."[47] While inspiration may guarantee the veracity of scripture, it does not necessarily guarantee veracity of interpretation. If the "revelations and lessons in Scripture are addressed to us personally and practically, the presence among us of a formal judge and standing expositor of its words is imperative." Thus, "the gift of inspiration requires as its complement the gift of infallibility." Hence, it follows that, once the "legitimate authority has spoken," subsequent resistance is an "act of heresy." But it also follows that until that authority speaks, it is not disloyalty to advocate a "contrary interpretation," provided it does not contravene faith or morals.[48]

Scripture possesses the "nature" of a sacrament.[49] Since the "formation of the sacred text" is a collaborative effort between God and certain individuals, it has a literal and a mystical sense.[50] God is the "*Auctor*" or "primary cause," and the individual is the "human *Scriptor*" or author.[51] It is not contrary to orthodoxy to think that some authors probably never understood the mystical dimension of their writing or were unaware of the presence of the Holy Spirit. Some were plagued with personal doubts and anxieties as Paul sometimes was. Occasionally, they even apologized about their literary shortcomings, as in Ecclesiasticus and 2 Maccabees.[52] Nor is it heresy to think that a canonical book is made up of "pre-existing documents" borrowed from secular uninspired sources. A book may be inspired even though not one word of it is an original document. For example, the first book of Ezra consists of "contemporary historical journals, kept from time to time by the prophets or other authorised persons, who were eye-witnesses for the most part of what they record, and whose several narratives were afterwards strung together, and either abridged or added to, as the case required, by a later hand, of course an inspired hand."[53] All that is required for a book to be canonical is an "inspired" editor, "authoritative in faith and morals, from whose fingers the sacred text passed."[54] Nor does it matter whether "one or two Isaiahs" may have written the book bearing that prophet's name, it is still inspired. Titles and authorship have nothing to do with inspiration.[55]

No divine gift is given indiscriminately; each is given for "precise and definite purposes." Inspiration is no exception. If Christian revelation discloses supernatural truths relevant to faith and morals and comes through scripture, what is more natural than to say that each writer had the gift of inspiration?[56] While Trent and Vatican I are emphatic concerning the link between inspiration, and faith and morals, "it is remarkable that they do not say a word directly as to its inspiration in matters of fact." It would be wrong, however, to conclude "that the record of facts in Scripture does not come under the guarantee of its inspiration . . . for this plain reason":

> . . . the sacred narrative, carried on through so many ages, what is it but the very matter for our faith, and rule of our obedience? what but that narrative itself is the supernatural teaching, in order to which inspiration is given? . . . Its pages breathe of providence and grace, of our Lord, of His work and teaching, from beginning to end. It views facts in those relations in which neither ancients, such as the Greek and Latin classical historians, nor moderns, such as Niebuhr, Grote, Ewald, or Michelet, can view them. In this point of view it has God for its author, even though the finger of God traced no words but the Decalogue. Such is the claim of Bible history in its substantial fulness to be accepted *de fide* as true. In this point of view, Scripture is inspired, not only in faith and morals, but in all its parts which bear on faith, including matters of fact.[57]

Notes

1. *Apo.*, p. 9.
2. *L.D.* I, 254.
3. *D.A.*, pp. 146; 234.
4. *Ibid.*, p. 146.
5. BOA A. 11. 12. Sermon 568 (18 Oct. 1840), untitled, pp. 2-3.
6. *Ibid.*, pp. 18-20.
7. Letter to Mrs W. Froude (8 Nov. 1840) *L.D. VII*, 435. "What the Apocrypha is to the Pentateuch, Prophets and Psalms," so are "Hebrews, Apocalypse, St James, 2 and 3 St John, 2 St Peter to the Gospels, Acts and Epistles." Furthermore, the Apocrypha "has not so much evidence as the Hebrews etc, etc,." and "that while we firmly believe the Hebrews etc, we do not think it safe to admit the Apocrypha."
8. BOA A.11. 2. "On the Connection in doctrine and statement of the Books of the Apocrypha with the New Testament."
9. *Ibid.*, p. 16.

10. *Ibid.*, pp. 17-8.

11. *Ibid.*, pp. 22; 24; 28; 32.

12. *Ibid.*, p. 33.

13. *Ibid.*, pp. 9-10.

14. Plenary inspiration means that the Bible is fully inspired in every word and deed from cover to cover. Although scripture is "plenarily inspired," the questions remain, "for what purposes, and in what way." Inspiration of scripture in all parts is one thing, inspiration in all matters is another (*S.E.*, pp. 61-2).

15. Letter to Henry Wilberforce (St James's Day, 1840). *L.D. VII*, 367.

16. Since he had placed himself under the protection of a divinely appointed, infallible authority, he felt that the weight of past difficulties had been lifted from his shoulders for good (*Apo.*, p. 238).

17. *L.D.* XIX, 50; Letter to Robert Monteith (29 May 1861). See chapter 6, pp. 88-91.

18. *Apo.*, p. 238.

19. *T.P.* II, 36.

20. *Ibid.*, p. 31.

21. *Ibid.*, p. 36.

22. *Ibid.*, p. 32.

23. *Ibid.*, p. 35.

24. B. Reardon, *From Coleridge to Gore*, p. 321. The seven authors were: Frederick Temple (1821-1902), Headmaster of Rugby; Rowland Williams (1817-70), Professor of Hebrew, St. David's Lampeter, Wales; Baden Powell (1796-1860), Savilian Professor of Geometry, Oxford; Henry Bristow Wilson (1803-88), Vicar of Great Staughton, Huntingdonshire; Charles Wycliffe Goodwin (1817-78), Egyptologist and only lay contributor; Mark Pattison (1813-84), Rector of Lincoln College, Oxford; Benjamin Jowett (1817-93), Regius Professor of Greek, Oxford.

25. [H. B. Wilson (ed.)], *Essays and Reviews*, pp. 14ff.; 94 ff.; 178ff.; 422ff.

26. *L.D.* XIX, 488. 1862-63 saw the appearance of the first two parts of *The Pentateuch and Book of Joshua Critically Examined* by John William Colenso (1814-83), Anglican bishop of Natal, questioning their authorship and historical accuracy. Asked about it, Newman admitted that "there are great critical difficulties as regards the text and history of the Old Testament." But they never troubled him since he became a Catholic, "because the Church had been so very silent about the inspiration and definite authority and use of Holy Scripture," and "because my faith is formed by what *she* has been guided to declare, not what I may have reasoned out from the sacred text." Colenso's book is *"much cry and little wool."* He seems to have said "nothing very formidable, and to be unaware that good part of it has been said before" (*L.D.* XX, 360).

27. *Ibid.*, pp. 482-3; 488. The essayists were, in fact, advocating a very moderate form of biblical criticism from Germany. See J. L. Altholz, *Anatomy of a Controversy: The Debate over "Essays and Reviews"* (Vermont, 1994).

28. These "Papers on Inspiration, 1861, 1863" were posthumously published in *The Theological Papers of John Henry Newman on Biblical Inspiration and on Infallibility* (1979).

29. The immediate reason was the Kingsley affair, but the prevailing climate of suspicion left him complaining about not having "elbow room" to write on the subjects of the day (*L.D.* XXI, 481; letter to T. W. Allies, 6 July 1864):

> . . . recollect the Duke of Wellington's saying that a great country cannot have a little war— nor can a great subject in theology. To touch on a subject is to be crude and misleading; it is to incur nearly all the censures which the Church uses of books, to be erroneous, next to

heresy, ill-sounding, scandalous, and temerarious. Already, as it is, I hear murmurs about my book, which may give me trouble. *This* is the main cause I cannot write—I have no wish at my age, to be involved in controversy, and to spend my strength in self defence. I think it very hard that I may not write under the antecedent concession that I am a fallible mortal, but that every turn of expression is to be turned into a dogmatic enunciation. Those who thus wish me to talk with the tongues, not of men, but "of angels," had better themselves have a little "charity." I say this even supposing I am wrong—but I am not conscious I am—but see what loss of time it is to prove *after all* that I am right! (*Ibid.*, p. 145; letter to Aubrey de Vere, 6 July 1864. See letter to Henry James Coleridge, 24 July 1864, p. 160).

30. *L.D.* XI, 280; *L.D.* XIX, 482; 488; *L.D.* XX, 360; *L.D.* XXI, 265. No official declaration on the inspiration of the sacred texts themselves was made until the first Vatican Council in 1870.

31. Giovanni Perrone, *Praelectiones Theologicae*, Vol. I, 179-80 (40th ed. Rome, 1888). Newman did believe in plenary inspiration. A moderate theologian, he defended the view that, until the Church had settled a theological issue, people have the right of debate, provided, of course, they were consistent with faith and morals and did not scandalize people. Private theological opinions must not be taught as "*de fide*" statements. This can often cause confusion and distress. The Church had not formally declared that the sacred books were inspired. But neither did it discourage its members from believing they were (*T.P.* II, 39-40).

32. BOA Sermon 568, pp. 2-3.

33. *T.P.* II, 59.

34. *Ibid.*, pp. 75-6.

35. *Ibid.*, pp. 66-7.

36. *Ibid.*, pp. 58-9.

37. *Ibid.*, pp. 59-60.

38. *Ibid.*, pp. 60-1.

39. *Ibid.*, p. 74.

40. *Ibid.*, p. 61.

41. *Ibid.*, pp. 61-2.

42. *Ibid.*, p. 62.

43. *Ibid.*, p. 63.

44. *Ibid.*, p. 75.

45. *Ibid.*, pp. 22-3.

46. *S.E.*, p.1. It seems that he wrote it in response to an earlier article titled "History, Criticism and the Roman Catholic Church," which was a response to the recent English edition of *Recollections of my Youth* by Joseph Ernest Renan (1823-92). It was published in *The Nineteenth Century*. Newman then wrote a second essay to answer criticism from a Dr Healy (1841-1914) of Maynooth, who thought that his interpretation of inspiration ran counter to Vatican I. Both essays are included in *Newman—On The Inspiration Of Scripture*, J. D. Holmes and R. Murray (eds.).

47. *Ibid.*, p. 7.

48. *Ibid.*, pp. 12-15.

49. *Ibid.*, p. 16.

50. *Ibid.*, p. 18.

51. *Ibid.*, pp. 8-9; 17-8. If anyone wants to "construe *auctor* as *author*, or *writer*," Newman argues, "let it be so—only, then there will be two writers of the Scriptures, the divine and the human" (*Ibid.*, p. 9).

52. *Ibid.*, pp. 20-1.

53. *Ibid.*, pp. 23-4. Newman is quoting from *A Dictionary of the Bible comprising its Antiquities,*

Biography, Geography, and Natural History, William Smith (ed.), Vol. I, Part 1 (London, 1863), p. 606.

54. *Ibid.*, pp. 24-5.

55. *Ibid.*, pp. 24-6.

56. *Ibid.*, p. 43.

57. *Ibid.*, pp. 11-2. In spite of such unequivocal statements that scripture is inspired from cover to cover in matters of faith and morals and in matters of fact as well, some, such as Healy of Maynooth, thought that Newman was inferring that there could be minor matters of fact (*obiter dicta*) which did not come under the umbrella of inspiration. *Obiter dicta:* a term probably borrowed from *Divinae Fidei Analysis* by Henry Holden (1592-1622), Paris, 1782, p. 82.

Newman and Some Twentieth-Century Theologies of Revelation

Twentieth-century theology has seen a much more systematic approach to revelation. Although Newman himself was never called upon to write a comprehensive study, his thinking was along the same lines as those adopted by Hans Urs von Balthasar, Karl Rahner, H. Richard Niebuhr, and others. Leaving aside other considerations, the Second Vatican Council seems to have taken on the heart and mind of Newman in this regard.

Collectively, the First Vatican Council's statements on revelation focussed on a deposit of faith entrusted to the Apostles by Christ and subsequently to the Church. Catholic theologians continued to focus on its propositional aspect. Pius X's condemnation of Modernism and his reaffirmation of revelation's objectivity perpetuated this approach. As a result, some of the more innovative ideas of individuals such as Möhler, Scheeben, Blondel, and Newman himself were temporarily eclipsed.[1]

By the 1940s, however, some Catholic theologians were recognizing that a fresh look at revelation was overdue. Once Pius XII gave his blessing to biblical scholarship, it was not very long before revelation came under the spotlight.[2] Even before 1943 there were Catholic scholars offering a wider perspective. For example, in 1936 Otto Karrer was arguing—possibly with the political situation in Germany in mind at the time—that, because of the richness and freedom of Christian revelation, "it is possible to recognise frankly and judge charitably the goodness and holiness to be found in any quarter without blinding ourselves to the defects of systems or individuals." There can be no "acceptable" Christian apologetic "which is not prepared to see with equal clarity what is good and what is less laudable in any religion and to appraise both with equal honesty." Christianity teaches that there is one God who is "Father, Redeemer and Sanctifier" of everyone of "good will":

It therefore does not compel us to hold, on the contrary it makes it impossible to hold, that all men living by accident of birth or upbringing before the Christian era or outside the visible sphere of Christianity are solely on that account a species of pariahs, disinherited from the Kingdom of Heaven and cast out by their Father for no personal fault—to hold that millions of men and women, indeed the vast majority of the human race, though created in God's image and likeness, have been so completely forsaken by Him that their search for God and their worship of Him are sheer illusion and empty show, their entire life a deceit. On the contrary, our religion teaches us that even "of these stones God can raise up children to Abraham," and there is no error which does not contain an element of truth; and it invites us to envisage the history of mankind as God's method of education, by which alike for the individual and the race the imperfect gradually prepares the way for the perfect and leads up to it. Christianity is inspired by the conviction that it is not destruction but "fulfilment." On that conviction it takes its stand, and without it would lose its exalted vocation, exercised in the spirit of Christ, to be the mother and teacher of the nations.[3]

In discussing the Alexandrian doctrine of the *Logos*, Hans Urs von Balthasar suggests that the "adoption and Christianisation of pagan wisdom" is no "profanation of divine wisdom." It is merely the "harvesting of what belonged originally to the true *Logos*" and can be understood only by returning it to its proper home. All "philosophy, mythology, and poetry" belong "rightfully" to Christ first and to people afterwards.[4] On no account should the multiple "paths that humanity has taken toward salvation" be seen as tricks of the devil. Nor should the "mind that conceived them" be "branded" idolatrous, even if these paths be "fragmentary and unable to provide total, objectively indivisible salvation." In inventiveness and practicality, they "represent the boldest conceptions and most exalted endeavours of the human spirit, borne through history by individuals and peoples prepared to sacrifice their lives for them."[5] They are "serious attempts" to discover salvation and "may contain redeeming grace hidden within them": "Since 'Adam' (that is, since the beginning of creation) and all the more since Christ, the world stands in the light of grace, nature as a whole is intrinsically finalised to supernature, whether it wants it or not, knows it or not. Natural knowledge of God, natural religious ethics stand under this sign, whose manifest character the Church proclaims. . . . Is not this the meaning of the old patristic doctrine of the 'logos spermatikos'?"[6]

According to Karl Rahner, prior to God's self-revelation in Jesus Christ, there already existed a universal, natural revelation, which is no less than the "presence of God" in the heart and mind of every individual—a presence in the form of a question to which Jesus Christ is the ultimate answer. Although anterior to the Incarnation, this natural revelation possesses the character of a historical event and is a permanent, universal, supernatural existential.[7] It is an authentic, transcendental experience of God's self-communication and claims a "history which is identical with the history" of the human race.[8] Unlike God's self-revelation in the person of Jesus Christ, natural revelation is a subjective event which takes place "in the depths of the spiritual person within the realm of consciousness" and includes everyone, everywhere, "because all are to be integrated into the single salvation of the single and total person." Therefore, "all transcendent subjectivity possesses itself not . . . *alongside* history, but *in* this very history, which is precisely the history" of human transcendence itself.[9] Thus, the Incarnation becomes the "only really tangible caesura in the universal history of salvation and revelation, and it enables us to distinguish a particular and official history of revelation within the universal history of revelation before Christ."[10]

The "culmination and final form" of God's self-revelation in Jesus Christ is "explicitly" present in a "socially constituted form" called the Church, which "receives and announces this absolute revelation." Insofar as this revelation is "definitive and victorious, and not merely ideological, but is really abidingly present in Christ, the Church is infallible in its confession of this truth":

> The objective and real truth of God's self-giving in Christ is present in its confession which cannot fail or err when it is done with the Church's absolute commitment. Otherwise the truth of Christ himself would no longer be present. Since this victorious character of Christ's truth is constitutive of the hierarchical Church, infallibility must belong to the hierarchical leadership of the Church, its magisterium (Pope and episcopate) in its function of service. Its role is to preserve the abiding presence of Christ's truth by actualizing and unfolding its truth for each successive moment of history.[11]

Like Newman, H. Richard Niebuhr also thought that Christianity possesses an internal and an external reality. One-world thinking, which focusses too much either on this world or the next, "has always betrayed Christianity into the denial of some of its fundamental convictions."[12] As surely as dualism constantly surfaces in philosophy, it also surfaces in history and religion. The question of "how to think in two-worldly terms," without concluding that a God of Good exists alongside a God of Evil, is an immensely important problem from which there is no "speculative escape." From "an objective inquiry into the life of Jesus to a knowledge of him as the Christ who is our Lord," there is "no continuous movement." Only a personal "leap of faith" can catapult a person "from observed to lived history."[13]

Though there is no "metaphysical or meta-historical solution" to the dilemma of historical dualism, there are ways of handling it positively. We may not be able to describe how internal and external "aspects of historical events are ultimately related," but we can focus on "their functional relationship." This must not be just a general statement of what all of us "ought to do," it should be a statement of "what we have found it necessary to do in the Christian community on the basis of the faith that is our starting point." Therefore, "beginning with internal knowledge of the destiny of self and the community," the Church must reflect on, learn from and respond to external views of itself which outsiders can see. For example, Karl Marx's view of Christianity may not reflect "*the*" whole truth about it, but the Church may recognize "*a* truth," unpalatable though this may be at the time.[14] Although it needs to reflect on "the revelatory moment in its own history," it would do well also to reflect on "all the events of time" in order to discern the "workings of one mind and will." The God of "inner history" is also the God of "external history." Because faith and sin are part of that history, the Church's "standpoint" will always be a "limited" one, but what it can learn from this vantage point is potentially limitless:

> Faith cannot get to God save through historic experience as reason cannot get to nature save through sense-experience. But as reason … can seek the evidence of a like pattern in all other experience, so faith … can and must look for the manifestation of the same self in all other events. Thus prophets, for whom the revelation of God was connected with his mighty acts in the deliverance of Israel from bondage, found the marks of that God's working in the histories of all the nations. The Christian community must turn in like manner from the revelation of the universal God in a limited history to the recognition of his rule and providence in all events of all times and communities.[15]

The revelation of Christ is an "intelligible event." It is "that part of our inner history which illuminates the rest of it" and "makes all other events intelligible."[16] Rather than being "contrary to reason," it signifies the "discovery of rational pattern" and the point at which we "begin to think and act as members of an intelligible and intelligent world of persons."[17] Whatever revelation means, it means an "event in our history which brings rationality and wholeness into the confused joys and sorrows of personal existence and allows us to discern order in the brawl of communal histories."[18] Through that unique event, we begin to "understand what we remember, remember what we have forgotten and appropriate as our own past much that seemed alien to us." The whole of history

> ... is potentially a single epic. In the presence of the revelatory occasion it can and must remember in tranquillity the long story of human ascent from the dust, of descent into the sloughs of brutality and sin, the nameless sufferings of untold numbers of generations, the groaning and travailing of creation until now—all that otherwise is remembered only with despair. There is no part of that past that can be ignored or regarded as beyond possibility of redemption from meaninglessness. And it is the ability of the revelation to save all the past from senselessness that is one of the marks of its revelatory character.[19]

Part of Newman's world view is based on a God, both immanent and transcendent, a revelation always mediated, a human nature not totally corrupt, a belief in revealed religion presupposing belief in natural religion, and a faith generating faith. By contrast, Karl Barth's world view is diametrically opposite. Barth maintained God to be absolutely transcendent and mysterious, revelation always immediate, and human nature without God to be totally corrupt.[20] In our orientation toward God, we are not just "sick," but "dead." By ourselves, we cannot even begin to speak with God or about God.[21] When revelation does occur, it is never the result of any initiative, "insight and skill" on our part. It happens only "in the freedom of God to be free for us," and to liberate us from our wicked ways.[22] Christian belief does not spring from a lower level of belief. It rises out of undiluted pagan unbelief. There is Christian belief and there is unbelief, and nothing in between.[23] Apart from the revelatory event of Jesus Christ, there is no natural religion, no universal revelation in philosophy, literature or theology. God is simply unknowable.[24] Human religions arrogantly "grasp at God," and their teaching ends up as the "contradiction of revelation" and the "concentrated expression of unbelief." Religion is "never true in itself and as such. The revelation of God denies that any religion is true, i.e., that it is in truth the knowledge and worship of God and the reconciliation of man with God. For as the self-offering and self-manifestation of God, as the work of peace which God Himself has concluded between Himself and man, revelation is the truth beside which there is no other truth, over against which there is only lying and wrong."[25]

People have often referred to Newman as the "Absent Father" of the Second Vatican Council and to the Council as his Council.[26] Some even see him as a prophet whose voice the assembly listened to, while others say that he would have disapproved of it.[27] Others again thought his influence exaggerated.[28] There is no doubt, however, that many bishops at the Council were influenced by Newman's ideas, though never explicitly acknowledging it at the time or since.[29] Indirect influence was obviously present. No argument or opinion can erode the fact that Newman's insights into the nature of the Church, theological development, personal conscience, the laity, universal revelation, the sacramental principle, and inspiration were at the heart of the Council's work.[30] Instead of re-endorsing Vatican I's legalistic approach to revelation, Vatican II took a "sacramental view," encompassing "law and grace, word and deed, message and sign," the "person and his utterance," the "universality of salvation" in Jesus Christ, who is the "sum total" of revelation.[31] Those who, "through no fault of their own," are unfamiliar with the "Gospel of Christ or his Church," but "seek God with a sincere heart," follow "the dictates of their conscience," will win eternal salvation. In fact, whatever elements of goodness are to be found anywhere, such truths are a "preparation for the Gospel and given by him who enlightens all men and women that they may at length have life."[32]

The human race is one community, has one origin, possesses one goal and looks to religion for answers to the "unsolved riddles of human existence." Thus, Hinduism seeks liberation from the "trials of the present life by ascetical practices, profound meditation, and recourse to God in confidence and love." Buddhism "testifies to the essential inadequacy of this changing world" by proposing a way of life by which people can "attain a state of perfect liberation and reach supreme illumination either through their own efforts or by the aid of divine love."[33] The Church encourages its own members, through dialogue, to recognize, preserve and promote all spiritual, moral truths and values in non-Christian religions.[34] Everything true and holy everywhere is a divine gift and must be preserved: "The Catholic Church rejects nothing of what is true and holy in these religions. It has a high regard for the manner of life and conduct, the precepts and doctrines which, although differing in many ways from its own teaching, nevertheless often reflect a ray of that truth which enlightens all men and women."[35]

In the task of evangelizing, sensitivity, flexibility, and adaptability to the customs and values of other religions and cultures must have priority as this work is "nothing else, and nothing less," than making Christ known. So, wherever there are "elements of truth and grace," they represent a "secret presence of God": "So whatever goodness is found in people's minds and hearts, or in the particular customs and cultures of peoples, far from being lost is purified, raised to a higher level and reaches its perfection, for the glory of God, the confusion of the demon, and the happiness of men and women everywhere."[36]

If then, in its early days, Christianity successfully assimilated the culture and thought of classical Greece and Rome, if it is still today what it has always been, if all authentic religions originate from the one, eternal truth, if Christ is already present, should not this pilgrim Church continue to broaden its horizons and be enriched by listening to and learning from the other great religions of the world?[37]

Notes

1. See G. Moran, *Theology of Revelation*, pp. 27-30.

2. *Divino Afflante Spiritu* (1943).

3. O. Karrer, *Religions of Mankind*, pp. 6-7. Karrer assisted Erich Pryzwara (1889-1969) in translating into German those writings of Newman's which best illustrated his philosophy of religion. They were published in 1922 under the title *Newman Christentum, Ein Aufbau aus seine Werken*, subsequently published in English as *A Newman Synthesis* in 1931, and later as *The Heart of Newman* in 1962 (reprinted San Francisco, 1997). Karrer also published an anthology of Newman texts on the Church under the title *Kardinal J. H. Newman: Die Kirche*, Volume I being published in 1945, Volume II in 1946. See W. Becker, "Newman's influence in Germany," in *The Rediscovery of Newman*, J. Coulson and A. M. Allchin (eds.).

4. H. U. von Balthasar, *Man in History*, pp. 160-1. See also *Love Alone: The Way of Salvation*, pp. 11ff.; *Word and Revelation*, pp. 108ff.

5. *Ibid.*, pp. 53-4. See W. Becker, *art. cit.*, p. 187.

6. H. U. von Balthasar, "In Retrospect," p. 198, from *The Analogy of Beauty*, J. Riches (ed.).

7. K. Rahner, *Foundations of Christian Faith*, pp. 170-1.

8. *Ibid.*, p. 153.

9. *Ibid.*, p. 172.

10. *Ibid.*, pp. 174-5.

11. K. Rahner, in *Sacramentum Mundi*, Vol. 5, p. 353.

12. H. R. Niebuhr, *The Meaning of Revelation*, pp. 82-3. See *Ess.* II, 190ff.

13. *Ibid.*

14. *Ibid.*, pp. 83-5.

15. *Ibid.*, pp. 86-7.

16. *Ibid.*, p. 93.

17. *Ibid.*, pp. 94-5.

18. *Ibid.*, p. 109.

19. *Ibid*, pp. 112-3.

20. In *A Brief Theology of Revelation* (1995), C. E. Gunton thinks that Barth's insistence on a God as revealed only through God "detracts from the incarnational and pneumatological mediation of revelation" (pp. 3-4).

21. K. Barth, *Church Dogmatics*, I, II, p. 257.

22. *Ibid.*, p. 65.

23. Ibid., p. 302.

24. Barth, *Church Dogmatics*, II, I, pp. 168; 170-2.

25. Barth, *Church Dogmatics*, I, II, p. 325. See "Barth's Theology of Revelation I—The Setting in Life," by Aidan Nichols, *Downside Review* (July 1994), pp. 153-63; "Barth's Theology of Revelation II—Theology and Church," by Aidan Nichols, *Ibid.*, (Jan. 1995), pp. 20-30.

26. Bishop Robert J. Dwyer, "Cardinal John H. Newman: 'Absent' Council Father," *The West Virginia Register* (17 Jan. 1966), p. 1; John Coulson, "If Newman were at the Council," *Search* (Jan. 1966), p. 324; Edward Kelly, *The Catholic World* (Feb. 1966), p. 291.

27. If anything, Newman was a "prophet" of the Council. In a letter to a Fellow of Trinity College, Oxford, Alfred Plummer (1841-1925), about the recent definition of infallibility, he wrote: "Let us have a little faith in her [the Church] I say. Pius [IX] is not the last of the Popes. The fourth Council modified the third, the fifth the fourth. . . . The late definition does not so much need to be undone, as to be completed. . . . Let us be patient, let us have faith, and a new Pope, and a reassembled Council may trim the boat" (C. S. Dessain, "Cardinal Newman as a Prophet," *Concilium* (Sept. 1968). For a different perspective, see M. Davies (ed.), *Newman Against the Liberals* (Devon, 1978).

28. For example, George Patrick Dwyer, archbishop of Birmingham at the time, wrote to the American Church historian, John Tracy Ellis on 4 Nov. 1975: "I wonder too if his [Newman's] influence on Vatican II has not been exaggerated. I attended the Council, of course, and as you rightly say development of doctrine was a fundamental principle in the Council's work but I never remember that Newman's own particular theory on development was quoted or used" (BOA N. Corr., Cause).

29. For example, James J. Hogan, bishop of Altoona-Johnstown, USA, wrote to Cardinal Palazzani, Prefect of the Congregation for the Causes of Saints, on 26 July, 1985: "As I attended the four sessions of the Second Vatican Council, I was not alone in the belief that the Holy Spirit saw to Cardinal Newman's spiritual and intellectual presence hovering over the Council. For me his spirit and legacy was almost visible, audible, tangible"(BOA N. Corr., Cause).

30. See Vincent Ferrer Blehl, S.J., "The Intellectual and Spiritual Influence of J. H. Newman," *Downside Review* (Oct. 1993), pp. 251-7. Nicholas Lash's statement that "Newman had little direct influence on what took place at Vatican II" needs qualifying ("Tides and Twilight: Newman since Vatican II," I. Ker and A. G. Hill (eds.), *Newman after a Hundred Years*, p. 464).

31. J. Ratzinger, "Revelation Itself," in *Commentary on the Documents of Vatican II*, H. Vorgrimler (ed.), Vol. 3, p. 171. Second Vatican Council, Dogmatic Constitution on Divine Revelation, *Dei Verbum*, 2.

32. Second Vatican Council, Dogmatic Constitution on the Church, *Lumen Gentium*, 16.

33. Raymond Panikkar (b. 1918) believes that, while Christianity and Hinduism may inhabit different doctrinal spheres, the same human being in the same "naked existence" still struggles to reach "fulness and perfection." Not only is Jesus Christ the crossroads where these two great religious traditions meet, he is probably "their only point of intersection." See J. Moltmann, "Christianity and the World Religions," in G. Hick and B. Hebblethwaite (eds.), *Christianity and other Religions*, pp. 208-9.

34. Hans Küng maintains that, without "peace between religions, war between the civilizations. No peace among the religions without dialogue between the religions. No dialogue between the religions without investigation of the foundations of the religions" (*Christianity*, 1994, p. 783).

35. Second Vatican Council, Declaration on the Relation of the Church to Non-Christian Religions, *Nostra Aetate*, 1-2.

36. Second Vatican Council, Decree on the Church's Missionary Activity, *Ad Gentes Divinitus*,

9. Bede Griffiths (1906-93) believes that the Church can no longer afford to ignore the "power, the influence, and the depth" of non-Christian traditions. It was a problem which the early Church successfully solved. If it is to reach its promised fulfilment in Jesus Christ, it must do the same today to Oriental religions, most of which are "older than Christianity" and "still stand with absolute firmness and show signs of growth rather than of disintegration." Although they are "two hemispheres" and represent "two totally different approaches" to ultimate truth, they are "complementary," and they both need each other. "Without Christianity I do not think the Oriental religions can answer the needs of the modern world. But without the enrichment of the mystical tradition of Asia I doubt whether the Western Churches can really discover the fullness of Christ. We have to meet and share" (B. Griffiths, *The Cosmic Creation: The Hindu Way to God*, London, 1983, pp. 25-6).

37. *Dev.*, pp. 355ff.; *D.A.*, pp. 210-1. In its principles of growth, continuity, assimilation and perennial vigour, Newman's *Essay on Development* has been described as a "manual of missionary adaptation" for taking the gospel into other cultures and religions. C. S. Dessain, "Newman's Philosophy and Theology," in D. J. De Laura (ed.), *Victorian Prose*, p. 176.

Select Bibliography

(All primary sources from the Birmingham Oratory Archives (BOA) have been quoted in footnotes throughout with full details and archival location numbers.)

1. General Studies of Newman's Life and Work

Biemer, G. *Newman on Tradition*, K. Smyth (trans.). London, 1967.

Blehl, V. F., S.J. *The White Stone: The Spiritual Theology of John Henry Newman*. Massachusetts, 1993.

Boekraad, A. J. *The Personal Conquest of Truth According to J. H. Newman*. Louvain, 1955.

Bouyer, L. *Newman: His Life and Spirituality*. London, 1958.

Chadwick, O. *From Bossuet to Newman*. Second edition, Cambridge, 1987.

Coulson, J. (ed.). *On Consulting the Faithful in Matters of Doctrine*. London, 1961.

Coulson, J. and A. M. Allchin (eds.). *The Rediscovery of Newman: An Oxford Symposium*. London, 1967.

Culler, A. D. *The Imperial Intellect: A Study of Newman's Educational Ideal*. New Haven, 1955.

De Laura, D. *Hebrew and Hellene in Victorian England: Newman, Arnold, and Pater*. Austin and London, 1969.

Dessain, C. S. *John Henry Newman*. Third edition, Oxford, 1980.

———. *Newman's Spiritual Themes*. Dublin, 1977.

Gilley, S. *Newman and his Age*. London, 1990.

Grave, S. A. *Conscience in Newman's Thought*. Oxford, 1989.

Holmes, J. D. and R. Murray, S.J. *On the Inspiration of Scripture; John Henry Newman*. London, 1967.

Ker, I. *The Achievement of John Henry Newman*. London, 1990.

———. *Healing the Wound of Humanity: The Spirituality of John Henry Newman*. London, 1993.

———. *John Henry Newman: A Biography*. Oxford, 1988.

———. *Newman: On Being a Christian*. London, 1990.

———. *Newman the Theologian: A Reader*. London, 1990.

Ker, I. and A. G. Hill (eds.). *Newman after a Hundred Years.* Oxford, 1990.

Lash, N. *Newman on Development: The search for an explanation in history.* London, 1975.

Louth, A. *Discerning the Mystery: An Essay on the Nature of Theology.* Oxford, 1983.

Merrigan, T. *Clear Heads and Holy Hearts: The Religious and Theological Ideal of John Henry Newman.* Louvain, 1991.

Pelikan, J. *Development of Christian Doctrine: Some Historical Prolegomena.* New Haven, 1969.

Selby, R. C. *The Principle of Reserve in the Writings of John Henry Cardinal Newman.* Oxford, 1975.

Seynaeve, J. *Cardinal Newman's Doctrine on Holy Scripture.* Louvain, 1953.

Sheridan, T. L. *Newman on Justification.* New York, 1967.

Strange, R. *Newman and the Gospel of Christ.* Oxford, 1981.

Thomas, S. *Newman and Heresy: The Anglican Years.* Cambridge, 1991.

Trevor, M. *Newman: The Pillar of the Cloud.* London, 1962.

———. *Newman: Light in Winter.* London, 1962.

Vargish, T. *Newman: The Contemplation of Mind.* Oxford, 1970.

Ward, W. *The Life of John Henry Cardinal Newman: Based on His Private Journals and Correspondence.* 2 volumes, London, 1913.

2. General Historical and Theological Background

Altholz, J. L. *The Liberal Catholic Movement in England: The "Rambler" and its Contributors 1848-1864.* London, 1962.

Balleine, G. R. *A History of the Evangelical Party in the Church of England,* London, 1908.

Brent, R. *Liberal Anglican Politics: Whiggery; Religion, and Reform 1830-1841.* Oxford, 1987.

Chadwick, O. *The Secularization of the European Mind in the Nineteenth Century.* Cambridge, 1975.

———. *The Victorian Church, Part 1.* Third edition, London, 1971.

———. *The Victorian Church, Part 2.* Second edition, London, 1972.

Corsi, P. *Science and Religion: Baden Powell and the Anglican Debate, 1800-1860.* Cambridge, 1988.

Elliott-Binns, L. E. *English Thought 1860-1900: The Theological Aspect,* London, 1956.

Forbes, D. *The Liberal Anglican Idea of History,* Cambridge, 1952.

Jay. E. (ed.). *The Evangelical and Oxford Movements.* Cambridge, 1983.

Macran, F. W. *English Apologetic Theology*. London, 1905.

Nichols, A., O.P. *The Panther and the Hind: A Theological History of Anglicanism*. Edinburgh, 1993.

Overton, J. H. *The English Church in the Nineteenth Century (1800–1833)*. London, 1894.

Prickett, S. *Romanticism and Religion: The Tradition of Coleridge and Wordsworth in the Victorian Church*. Cambridge, 1976.

Reardon, B. M. G. *From Coleridge to Gore: A Century of Religious Thought in Britain*. London, 1971.

Rowell, G. *The Vision Glorious: Themes and Personalities of the Catholic Revival in Anglicanism*. Oxford, 1983.

Smart, N. *et al.* (eds.). *Nineteenth Century Religious Thought in the West*. Vol. II, Cambridge, 1985.

Smyth, C. *Simeon and Church Order*. Cambridge, 1940.

Storr, V. F. *The Development of English Theology in the Nineteenth Century 1800–1860*. London, 1913.

Symondson, A. (ed.). *The Victorian Crisis of Faith*. London, 1970.

Walgrave, J. H. *Unfolding Revelation: The Nature of Doctrinal Development*, London, 1972.

Willey, B. *Nineteenth Century Studies: Coleridge to Matthew Arnold*. London, 1949.

———. *More Nineteenth Century Studies: A Group of Honest Doubters*. Cambridge, 1980.

3. Associated Literature

3.1. *Justin Martyr and Clement of Alexandria*

Bigg, C. *The Christian Platonists of Alexandria*. Oxford, 1886.

Chadwick, H. *Early Christian Thought and the Classical Tradition*. Oxford, 1966.

Daniélou, J. *Gospel Message and Hellenistic Culture*, John Austin Baker (trans.). London, 1973.

Ferguson, J. *Clement of Alexandria*. New York, 1974.

Frend, W. H. C. *The Rise of Christianity*. London, 1984.

Lilla, S. R. C. *Clement of Alexandria: A Study in Christian Platonism and Gnosticism*. Oxford, 1971.

Patrick, J. *Clement of Alexandria*. Edinburgh and London, 1914.

Saldanha, C. *Divine Pedagogy: A Patristic View of Non-Christian Religions*. Rome, 1984.

Tollinton, R. B. *Clement of Alexandria: A Study in Christian Liberalism*. 2 vols., London, 1914.

3.2.Bishop Joseph Butler

Butler, J. *The Analogy of Religion Natural and Revealed to the Constitution and Course of Nature,* W. E. Gladstone (ed.). Oxford, 1897.

————. *Sermons,* W.E. Gladstone (ed.). Oxford, 1897.

Collins, W. L. *Butler.* London, 1881.

Cragg, G. R. *From Puritanism to the Age of Reason: A Study of Changes in Religious Thought within the Church of England 1660 to 1700.* Cambridge, 1950.

Duncan-Jones, A. *Butler's Moral Philosophy.* London, 1952.

3.3. The Oxford Movement

Brilioth, Y. *The Anglican Revival: Studies in the Oxford Movement.* London,1925.

Church, R. W. *The Oxford Movement: Twelve Years 1833-1845.* London, 1900.

Härdelin, A. *The Tractarian Understanding of the Eucharist.* Uppsala, 1965.

4. Twentieth-Century Theologies of Revelation

Abraham, W. J. *Divine Revelation and the Limits of Historical Criticism.* Oxford, 1982.

Balthasar, H. U. von. *Word and Revelation: Essays in Theology, 1.* New York, 1964.

————. *Love Alone: The Way to Revelation—A Theological Perspective,* Alexander Dru (ed.). London,1963.

————. *Man in History: A Theological Study.* London, 1968.

————. *Word and Redemption: Essays in Theology, 2.* New York, 1965.

Barth, K. *Church Dogmatics,* Vol. I, second half-volume, "The Doctrine of the Word of God," G. W. Bromiley and T. F. Torrance (eds.). Edinburgh, 1956.

————. *Church Dogmatics,* Vol. II, first half-volume, "The Doctrine of God," G. W. Bromiley and T. F. Torrance (eds.). Edinburgh, 1957.

Brunner, E. *Revelation and Reason: The Christian Doctrine of Faith and Knowledge.* London, 1947.

Dulles, A. *Models of Revelation.* Dublin, 1983.

Gunton, C. E. *A Brief Theology of Revelation.* Edinburgh, 1995.

Hick, J. and B Hebblethwaite (eds.). *Christianity and Other Religions.* London, 1980.

Karrer, O. *Religions of Mankind,* E. I. Watkin (trans.). London, 1936.

Mascall, E. L. *The Openness of Being: Natural Theology Today.* London, 1971.

McDonald, H. D. *Theories of Revelation: An Historical Study 1860-1960.* London 1963.

Moran, G. *Theology of Revelation.* London, 1966.

Niebhur, H. R. *The Meaning of Revelation.* New York, 1962.

Rahner, K. *Foundations of Christian Faith: An Introduction to the Idea of Christianity.* London, 1978.

Riches, J. (ed.). *The Analogy of Beauty: The Theology of Hans Urs von Balthasar.* Edinburgh, 1986.

Rumscheidt, H. M. *Revelation and Theology: An Analysis of the Barth-Harnack Correspondence of 1923.* Cambridge, 1972.

Shorter, A. *Revelation and its Interpretation,* London, 1983.

Smart, N. *The Religious Experience of Mankind.* Glasgow, 1971.

Sykes, S. *The Identity of Christianity: Theologians and the Essence of Christianity from Schleiermacher to Barth.* London, 1984.

Ward, K. *Religion and Revelation.* Oxford, 1994.

Index of Names

Index of Subjects